T0340667

SpringerWienNewYork

TRACE
Transmission in Rhetorics,
Arts and Cultural Evolution
A Series by the Zurich University of the Arts (ZHdK)

Edited by
Gerhard Blechinger

Scientific Advisory Board
Thomas Grunwald
Martin Kurthen
Heiner Mühlmann

Stephan Trüby

Exit-Architecture
Design between War and Peace

With a Foreword by
Heiner Mühlmann

And a Project by
Exit Ltd.

Translated from the German by
Robert Payne

SpringerWienNewYork

Professor Stephan Trüby

© 2008 Springer-Verlag/Vienna • Printed in Austria
Springer-Verlag Wien New York is part of Springer Science+Business Media
springer.at

Copy editing: Nadja Schiller, ZHdK
Graphic design: Springer-Verlag, Vienna
Printed by: Ferdinand Berger & Söhne Ges.m.b.H., 3580 Horn, Austria

Printed on acid-free and chlorine-free bleached paper – TCF
SPIN: 12209064

with 23 figures

Bibliografische Information der Deutschen Nationalbibliothek
Die Deutsche Nationalbibliothek verzeichnet diese Publikation in der Deutschen Nationalbibliografie; detaillierte bibliografische Daten sind im Internet über http://dnb.d-nb.de abrufbar.

ISSN 1863-6411
ISBN 978-3-211-77969-9 Springer-Verlag Wien New York

Contents

Foreword

Heiner Mühlmann

What is showing-off?

Showing-off is display behaviour.

An example: Somebody gives a beggar alms and knows that a famous lady is watching him doing it. He was intending to give the beggar something anyway. Suddenly he realizes that the lady is watching him. He notices his behaviour changing and that he cannot help showing-off.

A communication system with two channels is the result. The first channel is the objective channel the only concern of which is that of the giver and the receiver of alms. The second channel is the display channel and it is here that the scene is transmitted to the onlooker.

I have borrowed the term 'display' from zoology, or to be more exact, ethology where it means 'behaviour altered by evolution which transmits information'. The great-crested grebe for example gathers nesting material with his bill and rises vertically in the water in front of the female. He has no intention of building a nest at this time. He is performing a nesting display with the message that he is ready to pair.

The triumphal arch for instance is purely a display building. It provides the excuse for an army to march through it, whereby the march serves no military purpose whatsoever, but is merely enacting a display of triumph for civilian onlookers. The objec-

1

tive channel of this parade relates to the logistics necessary in order to direct a military unit from A to B. The display channel transmits a message to the spectators.

The division of communication into a two-channel system can be clearly observed in rhetoric. Rhetorical systems offer elucidating insights into the organisational structures of cultures to which they belong.[1] Thus rhetoric in cultures influenced by Confucian thought differs significantly from that of Islamic cultures. The differential traits associated with Western rhetoric are typical of the organisational principles of Western culture. The most important differential trait is the two-channel structure and the display behaviour associated with it.

In Western culture only those who succeed in speaking on both the objective channel and the display channel can achieve any rhetorical effect. The objective channel is concerned with the semantic and unambiguous correctness of language, i.e. it is concerned with the 'content' of the speech. The display channel, on the other hand, is much more concerned with the 'manner' the speech is delivered in. Instantly recognizable phrases such as proverbs, quotations from poetry and songs are used here. It is here that language becomes 'figurative'. 'Figurative' means in fact that rhetorical figures are used. A rhetorical figure is a violation against the rules of the objective channel. Rules pertaining to grammar, semantics and unambiguity are breached. In other words, ordinary language is metabolised, but the metabolisms arising in this manner follow rules which the hearers are all familiar with.

---

[1]   Cf. George A. Kennedy: *Comparative Rhetoric. An Historical and Cross-Cultural Introduction*, New York: Oxford University Press, 1998.

In order to describe the relationship between the objective channel and the display channel I introduce the term 'hyper-reference'. The semantic and unambiguous correctness of the objective channel functions as a simple reference and or as a simple linguistic reference to reality. Here accuracy is called for. The display channel is concerned with the 'manner' the speech is delivered in. Here appropriateness is the order of the day. The reader registers these rules and asks himself: "What does the manner have to be appropriate for?" The answer to the question "Appropriate for what?" is provided by the second reference or hyper-reference.

The appropriateness of the 'manner' is not only determined by the ranking of the subject matter, but also the ranking accorded to the speaker, the ranking of the venue and the ranking of the location where the speech is delivered. In this context one differentiates between 'high ranking' and 'low ranking'. Similarly the means of expression are also classified into 'high ranking' and 'low ranking'.

In the classical period of Western rhetoric the ranking of appropriateness was called *decorum* and two styles were differentiated, the elevated style (Greek: *hypsos*; Latin: *sublimis*) and the humble style (Greek: *tapeinos*; Latin: *humilis*).[2] The elevated style, and here we come to the rule of appropriateness, was only permitted to be used when dealing with cultural matters of state sovereignty (Latin: *maiestas*), decisions pertaining to war and the fate of its warriors. The humble style could only be used in dealing with matters of economy or the family. In addition the humble style was prescribed for all things in the spheres of comedy, entertainment, love and erotic.

---

[2] Cf. Platon: *Gorgias*, p. 59; Aristoteles: *Rhetorica*, 3,7,1; Cicero, *De Oratore*, 3,55,210; Quintilian: *Institutio oratoria*, 11,1,1-93.

Rhetoric provided a system of rules which assigned appropriate means of expression for all content. This system of rules was evaluated and the rules were adjusted according to their ranking. In this context we speak of rule adjustment systems.[3] However, it should be noted that rule adjustment systems are the result of natural evolutionary processes. What is to be assessed as high ranking or sublime *decorum* and as low ranking is a consequence of what practices are adopted by one's ancestors.

As a result of evolutionary processes rule adjustment systems differ from families of rules which derived from norms. These families of rules could be termed 'rule standardization systems'. Laws, 'synthetically' created by legislators, belong to this category. It must be provable that laws can be correctly derived from the norms of a constitution. Rules stemming from rule standardization systems are artificial whereas laws of nature evolve by means of rule adjustment systems.

The difference between rules or laws which arise by natural means and rules or laws which are created artificially is the topic of the book *Gerechtigkeit als Zufall* (*Justice as Coincidence*) by Fabian Steinhauer which devotes itself to the problem of the history of law and evolutionary theory.[4]

The rule adjustment system of rhetoric reveals the following: The rule which says "If you speak of the horrors of war you must make use of the rhetorical figures belonging to the elevated style!" has a higher ranking than the rule that says "If you speak of the amorous problems of the shepherd Fido you must use rhetoric figures belonging to the humble style!" This

---

[3]   Cf. John H. Holland: *Adaption in Natural and Artificial Systems*, Cambridge, Mass.: The MIT Press, 1992.

[4]   Fabian Steinhauer: *Gerechtigkeit als Zufall. Zur rhetorischen Evolution des Rechts*, Vienna/New York: Springer, 2007.

means that the rules which have been evaluated as being low have to do the preliminary work for the rules which have been evaluated as being high. A rule adjustment system taken as a whole always serves the highest evaluated rule. It is a bucket brigade system in which everybody is doing the preliminary work for the person at the end of the line who pours the water on the fire by passing a bucket of water.[5]

We now come to a particular example of display behaviour which due to the principle of highest evaluation can be regarded as a main differential trait of Western culture. In the veritable cornucopia of rhetorical figures such as synedoches, ellipses, oxymorons, syncopes, metaphors, litotes, metonyms and so on and so on, there is one which cannot be overlooked and occupies the highest position in the rule adjustment system of rhetoric. Thereby Western culture to a certain extent makes a statement about itself. It announces a rule which declares: "This display behaviour is for me, for Western culture and matters of greatest importance." The rhetorical figure in question has the Greek name *aposiopesis* or in Latin *reticentia*. This figure may only be used in situations where the content involves something terrible. What is meant is the horror with which individuals are faced when they are plunged into borderline situations where they are expected to participate in the future triumph of their community. Where they have to do things which they would rather flee from. These activities leave irrevocable marks in the emotional memory. The emotional memory is also know as the 'nondeclarative memory'. Its contents are not marked with declarative symbols which enable them to be brought to mind at will. They are instead awakened by returning to the 'scene of the crime' or by images of the same which happen to appear in the imagination.

---

[5]   Cf. Holland, *Adaption in Natural and Artificial Systems*.

5

What is the *aposiopesis*, and how is it triggered off? The *aposiopesis* is breaking off a speech. This must be carried by the speaker, let us not forget that we are in the middle of display behaviour, so that the listener has the impression that the speaker is emotionally so overcome by the unbearable intensity of the subject matter that he is suffering from a fit of giddiness.

While dealing with the subject of 'actio', which means more or less 'gesture and body language', Quintilian advises the student of rhetoric to rumple the toga as a sign of his agitation, and to let the toga slip from his shoulders so that it has to be caught in his hands, immediately before implementing *aposiopesis*.[6] All this lends an air of helplessness to the speaker. The imposing silhouette of the toga wearer is lost and is replaced by the speaker standing there, looking like a bird with drooping wings, supporting his toga in his outstretched arms.

In order to transfer the emotion 'horror', by which the speaker is apparently overcome, to the listeners with the aid of *aposiopesis*, the following technique is used: The speaker should allow an image of the place where these horrors occurred to appear in his mind.[7] Thus the emotion which he is supposed to be transferring is awakened in him and after this has been achieved can be transferred empathetically to the listeners.

The speaker stands before his listeners. He has stopped speaking. He appears helpless with his toga hanging from his arms and it is obvious that he has been seized with dread.

The *aposiopesis* is the display of uninhibited emotional showmanship. The evaluating rules for appropriateness not only per-

---

[6]   Cf. Cicero, *De Oratore*, 3,56; Quintilian, *Institutio oratoria*, 11,3.
[7]   Cf. Quintilian, *Institutio oratoria*, 6,2,29.

mit this unrestrained behaviour but in fact prescribe it. The rhetorical rule adjustment system promotes this rule to the highest ranking rule which must be served by all the other rules. Thus the entire system of rhetoric focuses on this one isolated rule. At the same time *decorum* or the rule adjustment system emphasizes that this rule may only be implemented exceedingly rarely. It is in fact conceivable that it will never be used by a speaker in his whole career, simply because there was never the appropriate opportunity to put it to use. In addition teachers of rhetoric point out that triggering off the *aposiopesis* can often go wrong and that the speaker can risk making a laughing stock of himself. Nevertheless the system of rhetoric, with its display ranking, is gauged to this highest of rules.

Whoever has mastered *aposiopesis* and can also cater for good humour using the lower rhetorical modes can be considered rhetorically competent.

Evaluated emotional uninhibitedness does not only occur in rhetoric. Without this display behaviour the dramaturgy of tragedy would not work. It is indispensable for musical declamation of texts and it is just as indispensable for the portrayal of emotion and pain in painting.

If we assume that with evaluated uninhibitedness we have found a primary differential trait of Western culture, then it is only natural that we should wish to use this differential trait for comparative purposes in other cultures. We would like to answer the question as to whether this display behaviour is to be found in non-Western cultures, for example in cultures influenced by Confucianism. If it is considerably rarer or does not occur at all, then we would have found a significant cultural difference. It is conceivable that in rule adjustment systems influenced by Confucianism, referred to as 'rites' in Western literature, that evaluated uninhibitedness was never permitted because it would have been associated with permanent loss of face.

If we wish to use 'evaluated uninhibitedness' for the comparison of cultures mere suppositions about this behaviour, which can only be gained from hermeneutic interpretation, are not sufficient. This is because it is doubtful that the language of hermeneutics which we use has been obtained from our own culture. In other words, if one's own culture with its rule adjustment systems purports something to be of great importance, it does not necessarily mean that it is the most important element in the organization of that culture. Therefore it is essential in matters of cultural comparison that we can fall back on reliable data and a truly intercultural language.

Our research group TRACE based in Zurich is currently involved in obtaining reliable data and developing an intercultural language by experiments in the field of neuroscience. TRACE is a research project with the participation of the ZHdK (Zurich University of the Arts) and the Swiss Centre for Epilepsy. I can only say at this point in time that the experiments carried out up to now are very promising.

As far as the intercultural language is concerned, if we are able to describe cultural phenomena with neuroanthropological means then we have the culturally independent system of description that we seek at our disposal.

Which the important differential traits are, for a culture, can only be ascertained through the comparison of cultures. What we need in order to compare cultures are, (1) a knowledge, or more precisely a knowledge of data that has not been obtained by hermeneutic cultural introspection and (2) an intercultural system of description. It is only the experimental neurosciences than can supply these. Therefore there is no other alternative than a neuroanthropological approach when we are dealing with improving the effectiveness of cultural studies.

TRACE is also the name of the series of publications in which this book, which you now hold, is appearing. It is not only the name of a series of publications but at the same time the horizon from which Stephan Trüby's book on architecture attains its contours.

Exit-Architecture describes the locations where the display of uninhibitedness might occur. It also describes the locations which could trigger off the *aposiopesis* display as visions.

Stephan Trüby's book leads us from the *decorum* architecture of antiquity, through the defensive corridors of earlier modern times and then on through the corridors inside hospitals and apartments of the 19th century to the pervasive architecture of the 21st century. And in doing this, a central theme of architectural paranoia, risk management and threat assessment comes to the fore.

The 'safe space' of the future according to Trüby will be defined by gadgets. These gadgets will be in our clothing, will open the doors to the cybersphere. They will know everything about us and about the people in our proximity. They will tell us where we are and whether the place in question is safe. The safety that we so crave will result from continually observing each other and because we will know that we ourselves are being watched we will become reluctant show-offs. Our behaviour will change. We will develop a permanent display behaviour and according to Trüby a new *decorum* of the gadget and cybersphere will be the result.

Furthermore what will become obvious is that the two-channel communication system with its division into an objective channel and a display channel finds its perfect counterpart in architecture. Trüby presents the terms 'building codes' versus 'design codes', the former being the architectural counterpart of the objective channel and the latter of the display channel.

Exit-Architecture is a book about architecture and an architect's book: Stephan Trüby is a Professor of Architecture. However, *Exit-Architecture* is in contrast to other architect's books an altruistic work. Whereas most books of this ilk normally consider all things architectural and normally one's own architecture, Trüby is more interested in the paths which arise when they are encapsulated in architecture and not the architecture itself. These paths are worthy of our interest as they can give us insight into cultural organisation in its most important areas.

Trüby's description of the world's most conspicuous cultural path is breathtaking. This is the route leading pilgrims to Mecca via the place of the display 'the stoning of the devil' and the places of animal sacrifice. The extreme emotional behaviour of the people which can be observed there suggests that in the case of the three monotheistic religions, as Peter Sloterdijk describes in his latest book *Gottes Eifer*, that we are dealing with a cultural family.[8] Not only do they have monotheism in common but also culturally organised extreme emotions. It is likely that the cultural differences between the family of three, i.e. Judaism, Islam and Christianity and Confucianism are greater than among the members of the first named group. But the conflict existing between these three seems to be greater although the differences are slighter. One might assume the conflicts could be explained by the similarities and among these similarities is the display of evaluated uninhibitedness.

---

[8]   Cf. Peter Sloterdijk: *Gottes Eifer. Vom Kampf der drei Monotheismen*, Frankfurt am Main: Verlag der Weltreligionen im Insel Verlag, 2007.

Acknowledgements

Some of the following considerations arose in 1999 during my stay at the British School in Rome made possible by the Nick Boas Scholarship from the AA School of Architecture. I would especially like to thank the Boas family and the AA for creating this scholarship. Some of the chapters and passages represent revised versions of lectures and earlier publications which were made possible by Sandra Bartoli, Gerhard Blechinger, Rafael Horzon, Jean-Baptiste Joly, Nikolaus Kuhnert, Silvan Linden, Hans Ulrich Obrist, Yana Milev, Florian Schneider, Frank Werner and Olaf Winkler to mention but a few names. I am indebted to them as well the following people who have provided useful advice: Jonathan Allen, Shumon Basar, Matthias Böttger, Friedrich von Borries, Gerd de Bruyn, Martin Burckhardt, Noam Chomsky, Beatriz Colomina, Douglas Coupland, Diedrich Diederichsen, Benjamin Engelhardt, Rainer Fischbach, Julian Friedauer, Stephan Henrich, Daniel Hundsdörfer, Janice Kerbel, Martin Knöll, Wilfried Kühn, Sebastian Lippert, Ferdinand Ludwig, Mona Mahall, Iassen Markov, Dick Martini, Jürgen Mayer H., Daniel Mock, Achmed Rasch, Kersten Schagemann, Claus Schaible, Madelon Vriesendorp and Mark Wigley. I would also like to thank Tina Hartmann, Markus Miessen and Nadja Schiller who read the manuscript, made comments and suggested improvements. Last but not least I would especially like to express my gratitude to Robert Payne for his translation and Heiner Mühlmann whose initiative and support were indispensable in writing this book.

1. Ex-Architecture/Exit-Architecture: On Stress, Memoactivity and Cultural Transmission

„*We shape our buildings, and afterwards our buildings shape us.*"
Winston Churchill

If architects have a favourite sentence then this is it. Mantra-like it sounds when founding stones are laid, at topping-out ceremonies and the handing over of keys: *We shape our buildings, and afterwards our buildings shape us. We shape our buildings, and afterwards our buildings shape us. We shape our buildings...*

What is less known is the context in which Churchill said this: In the middle of the Second World War on 28th October 1943 a debate was raging in the British parliament on the question of whether the chamber of the House of Commons, which had been destroyed by German bombs in 1941, should be rebuilt exactly like the original [Fig. 1]. The Prime Minister insisted on having the room restored to its old form: "We shape our buildings, and afterwards our buildings shape us. Having dwelt and served for more than forty years in the late Chamber, and having derived very great pleasure and advantage therefrom, I, naturally, should like to see it restored in all essentials to its old form, convenience and dignity."[1]

In the light of day there could be no talk of 'convenience', and Churchill was aware of this. Long before the Second World War the Commons Chamber had become much too cramped to offer all the members of Parliament a comfortable seat. Why then did

---

[1] Winston Churchill, "The Churchill Centre" (http://www.winstonchurchill.org/i4a/pages/index.cfm?pageid=388; 19 July 2007).

Fig. 1: Steeped in memories: Winston Churchill in the bombed ruins of the House of Commons, London 1941.

the Prime Minister nevertheless insist on its exact reconstruction? In critical times, and this was his argument, a council chamber bursting at the seams was in Great Britain's own interest. A dramaturgy of the throng emphasized the urgent problems of state. Parliamentarians, squeezed into doorways and

aisles, in order to catch a glimpse into the overcrowded de-
bating chamber would, according to Churchill, guarantee an
appropriate "sense of crowd and urgency". Giles Gilbert Scott,
the architect who was commissioned with the rebuilding, made
only minor alterations for this very reason. Five years after the
end of the war the Commons Chamber was finally opened in all
its former glory. Not despite but *because* of its cramped conditions was it reconstructed.

The story makes us prick up our ears. Does architecture only
shape us when there is some kind of snag? When something
does not fit? Does the architects' favourite sentence apply to, of
all things, buildings which have become dysfunctional?

The question is, in its most general and condensed form: What,
as a special case of cultural transmission, is architectonic
transmission?

Initially, transmission can be defined as a success in learning
which is permanently adopted in its own behavioural reper-
toire and then transferred to the next generation. For example, among farmers in Normandy there is the puzzling tradition
that the father takes his firstborn son on his seventh birthday
for a walk around the perimeter of his land. At each corner of
the border the birthday boy suddenly gets his ears boxed. In
this way many generations of fathers have, not only unhappy
memories of their birthday, but also strong emotional ties to the
property they were later to inherit. The initiation ritual is like a
punch guaranteeing high stability.[2]

The terrain, which is staked out by such wanderings, is im-
printed where memories have proved to be especially memoac-

---

[2]   Cf. Clotaire Rapaille: *Der Kultur-Code*, Munich: Riemann, 2006, p. 34.

tive; i.e. in the episodic memory. This develops at the age of three to four and is the only memory system which is able to live through past experience. With this we possess a cognitive tool which can summon *tempi passati* into the here and now. In contrast to the type of memory which stores semantic content ('declarative memory') the episodic memory does not only remember the content but also where this was learnt.[3]

'Stress' is the driving motor for the episodic memory. In contrast to trauma which has as an amnesic effect, a stress event is fundamentally memory facilitating. 'Stress' is the term given to physiological process, which due to increased adrenalin, noradrenaline and cortisol secretion leads to a weakening of the metabolism, the immune system and in addition in the case of sexually mature humans – to sexual activity being curbed. Above all 'stress' means that all available energy reserves are focused so that they can be reserved for those motor, cognitive and neural functions that will be required by the body in a fight or flight situation. Of vital importance here is the central 'control box' of the limbic system, the hippocampus. Not only is the hippocampus responsible for spatial orientation but also for the cognition of anything new. Furthermore in the case of stress events it activates its sensitive neighbour: the amygdala. The latter is largely responsible for the arising of fear and panic and ensures long term memory in the case of learning content of a highly emotional nature.

Our understanding of the episodic memory is however too insufficient in order to explain transmission. Sociality analyses are considered the greatest of challenges in brain research.

---

[3]   Cf. Harald Welzer and Hans J. Markowitsch: "Reichweiten und Grenzen der interdisziplinären Gedächtnisforschung", in: Harald Welzer and Hans J. Markowitsch (eds.): *Warum Menschen sich erinnern können. Fortschritte der interdisziplinären Gedächtnisforschung*, Stuttgart: Klett-Cotta, 2006, p. 11.

At present there are hardly any technical possibilities to track down the neural correlates of interactions.[4] Brain research is not yet a real-time science in the turmoil of everyday conflict and cooperative behaviour. It generally focuses on the heads of individuals. Thereby it is well-known that the brain's development is not an autonomous biological process but rather the product of processes involving social exchange. It is the contact with others that shapes the neural switches.[5] The brain therefore must be considered the most flexible and incomplete organ that evolution has ever come up with: "No other living organism possesses anywhere near such neuroplasticity, no other brain is so undeveloped at birth as the human brain, no other has so much potential to adapt to different and changing environments."[6]

As long as mere individuals are its most significant epistemic subjects, will neuroscience not be able to remain the only reference science of cultural transmission analysis – this has also been realized by supporters of memetics. But their enterprise is a genetics lookalike competition without having any chance. Since while a DNA molecule actively copies itself during cell division in a fertilized egg cell – thus voluntarily or involuntarily passing itself on to the next generation – in the field of cultures no such replicator à la 'gene' can be isolated. Daniel Dennett's borrowed point where a scholar is only a librarian's way of creating another scholar,[7] is only half as precise in terms of evolutionary theory as Samuel Butler's *bon mot* of a hundred years before: "A hen is only an egg's way of making another egg."[8]

---

[4] Ibid.
[5] Cf. Harald Welzer: *Das kommunikative Gedächtnis. Eine Theorie der Erinnerung*, Munich: Beck, 2002, p. 222.
[6] Welzer, *Das kommunikative Gedächtnis*, p. 58.
[7] Daniel Dennett: *Darwin's Dangerous Idea*, London: Penguin, 1995, p. 202.
[8] Samuel Butler: *Life and Habit*, 1877.

Although memetics labours along because it is still lacking any evident 'smallest unit', its primary aim, the Darwinization of cultural theory,[9] definitely succeeds in being convincing. But it is not so much Darwin's ideas of natural selection but more his approach of thinking in populations which points the way to the future of a cultural theory as a hard science.[10] There are, for example, populations of Wagnerians, Corvette drivers, Shiites and Danes. Even a population of Danish Shiites who always drive on their pilgrimage to Bayreuth in Corvettes is conceivable under certain cultural evolutionary conditions. As long as suitable sets of data are available – sales figures for products, attendance at religious rituals, demographic information etc. – such groupings are ascertainable quantitatively. And this, after transfer of traits to students or children, over many generations. Via a round-about route of collective perspective a model for discrete cultural replicators can certainly be deduced which does not embarrass itself genetically speaking. This is the background in front of which Heiner Mühlmann proposes as the basic unit of cultural theory an atom-like abstraction called 'TU' ('transmission unit').[11]

What however sets transmissions in motion? And what is meant by 'culture' in the first place? "Culture is a dynamics of transmission."[12] Mühlmann's minimal definition says that only that

---

[9]   On the "Darwinization of cultural theory" see Robert Aunger (ed.): *Darwinizing Culture: The Status of Memetics As a Science*, Oxford/New York: Oxford University Press, 2001.

[10]   Cf. Robert Boyd and Peter J. Richerson: *The Origin and Evolution of Cultures*, Oxford/New York: Oxford University Press, 2005, p. 420.

[11]   According to Mühlmann, the 'TU' can appear in different 'states of aggregation' as commodity artefact ('ETU'; 'economic transmission unit'), as cultural transmisison unit ('CTU'; 'cultural transmission unit') and as commodity artefact with cultural results ('CETU'; 'culture-economic transmission unit'); cf. Heiner Mühlmann: "The Economics Machine", in: Igmade (eds.): *5 Codes: Architecture, Paranoia and Risk in Times of Terror*, Basel/Boston/Berlin: Birkhäuser, 2006, p. 232.

[12]   Heiner Mühlmann: *The Nature of Cultures. A Blueprint for a Theory of Cultural Evolution*, Vienna/New York: Springer, 1996, p. 98.

which transfers its distinguishing traits to the next generation at least once, can be regarded as culture. Thus culture has very little to do with the statics of architectural monuments and other 'enduring values' but rather with "stability of the transgenerational memory".[13] In Mühlmann's theories a theoretical figure called 'Maximal Stress Cooperation' (MSC) acts as the initial spark for the creation of all cultures. "'MSC' is stress-cooperation as a matter of life or death."[14] MSC events are exemplified by acts of war such as the Battle of Salamis, the Siege of Vienna or D-Day. They all led to cooperative stimuli amongst those who witnessed it. MSC events function as 'enculturation' meaning that behavioural differences will be copied within the same generation ('horizontal') and on to the next generation ('vertical').

The MSC theory gauges culture to its apparent counterpart, war. Culture, according to Mühlmann, "produces symptoms which can be measured in the form of difficulties in adapting; crime statistics, racism, civil war, fundamentalism; briefly, in the form of conflicts which leave signs that can be measured".[15] Here we have a specifically German tradition whereby 'culture' is in antagonism to 'civilization'. However with a decisive and provoking break, the roles of the good cop and bad cop have been switched. Immanuel Kant, on observing the "civilization" at the French court, advocates the "true virtue" of "culture", which he contrasts with "civilizedness" and its "deceiving, superficial courtesies";[16] Mühlmann however, with an eye to religious and ethnic-political conflicts from former Yugoslavia to Iraq, advocates a civilizing taming of the wild beast 'cul-

---

[13] Heiner Mühlmann: *MSC. The Driving Force of Cultures*, Vienna/New York: Springer, 2005, p. 6.

[14] Mühlmann, *The Nature of Cultures*, p. 36.

[15] Ibid., p. 88.

[16] Immanuel Kant, quoted after Norbert Elias: *Über den Prozeß der Zivilisation. Sozio-genetische und psychogenetische Untersuchungen*, Vol. 1, Frankfurt am Main: Suhrkamp, [18]1993, p. 10.

ture'.[17] Both the civilizing domestication of culture as well as its converse enculturation are applicable to the observations of transmission theory. And by 'observation' is definitely meant 'higher order observation' in the sense of systems theory. But in contrast to Niklas Luhmann's scepticism concerning 'ultimate observations'[18] the transmission theory, strengthened by neuroscience, refuses to give up hope of perceiving reality – and especially *cultural* reality.

The initial question aimed at the mechanisms of architectonic transmission can now be answered satisfactorily. Here we should differentiate between three cases; firstly the architecture which is 'simply standing around', secondly architecture which has been renovated, redeveloped or reconstructed, and thirdly the transmission of rules, laws, conventions and codifications.

By 'case 1' is meant the simple fact that architecture normally remains standing and usually longer than one single generation. Pieces of real estate stand like towers of strength of transgenerational dynamics whether the offspring want it or not. However, for the purposes of research into architectonic transmission this case is strictly to be excluded since it includes also forgotten architecture which is literally dead and buried. Ruins and sunken cities can only become components of considerations in transmission theory when there are brains that invest them with some kind of sense.[19]

---

[17] Cf. Mühlmann, *The Nature of Cultures*, p. 7.

[18] Cf. Detlef Krause: *Luhmann-Lexikon*, Stuttgart: Lucius & Lucius, ³2001, p. 111.

[19] On the culture genetics of ruins see Heiner Mühlmann: *Kunst und Krieg – Das säuische Behagen in der Kultur (Heiner Mühlmann über Bazon Brock)*, Cologne: Salon, 1998, p. 74.

It is with 'case 2' that the transmission theory comes into play. This case includes all situations where specific architectures are not left to their own devices but are excavated, maintained, taken care of or rebuilt: renovations, restorations, facility management, reconstructions etc. It should be pointed out that the differences between restoration and reconstruction are by no means as clear as preservationists would have us believe.

'Case 3' however proves itself to be the transmission with the most consequences and the following analysis will be devoted to it. In contrast to 'case 2' it is not about anything specific but rather something generic, something that is hardly visible but for this very reason shapes the more strongly. And in contrast to 'case 1' it is not concerned with the gradual, harmless and quiet end of buildings without witnesses, but rather with the numerous moments where architecture releases strong collective emotions and above all in the situations where danger, collapse and destruction threaten. This is because, and this also applies to architecture, the best chances for transmission involve situations characterized by their proximity to events involving stress (i.e. proximity to the greatest possible extremes) but at the same time always remain below the traumatic threshold of stress in a population. Thus war becomes the fulcrum on which evolutionary observations of architectonic culture are based.

This may well seem initially puzzling. War as the *constructor* of architecture? Is not war much more the *destroyer* of the same? Is not architecture fundamentally a peaceful activity? Doesn't it mean well with us – warmth and a roof over our heads? We are not dealing with bellicosity nor are we concerned here with disproving the glad and obvious tidings that there is nothing beneficial about wars. But it refers to the realization that architectonic evolution is inseparable from thrusts of innovation caused by war, new weapon technology and poststress achievements in codification. War is just as omnipresent in the pre-modern treatises on columns as in the modern standardization of building. It is just as present in the aesthetics of stealth and camouflage as in the always-happy-to-reconstruct terrains of the "Methuselah plot".*

Despite all the talk about the 'collective memory of the city', mnemonics has indeed contributed a lot to building, but building has contributed very little to mnemonics. Adrian Forty is right when in reference to Aldo Rossi's misunderstandings of Maurice Halbwachs he writes: "'Memory' may well yet prove to be a short-lived architectural category – and one inherently alien to architecture."[20] Architecture's collapse, whether caused by war or otherwise, has proved to be especially memoactive in fact.

As long ago as Cicero's account of the legend of origins of the Ars memoriae do we hear of the birth of mnemonics out of a cloud of dust of a building that had been destroyed: There was once a man called Simonides of Ceos who gave a speech at an evening banquet held by the host Scopas. The hired speaker not only eulogized the gentleman in question but also the twin gods Castor and Pollux, with the result that the frugal Scopas refused to pay Simonides the full amount. The host suggested that he collects the rest of his fee from the twins he had praised. Some time later the speaker, who had been cheated, was asked to come outside by two mysterious figures – apparently Castor and Pollux. Suddenly the building collapsed behind him. The banquet victims were so disfigured that none of them could be

---

* The term "Methuselah plot" refers to the 2004 bestseller *Das Methusalemkomplott. Die Macht des Alterns*, written by the German journalist Frank Schirrmacher [translator's note].

[20] Adrian Forty: *Words and Buildings. A Vocabulary of Modern Architecture*, New York: Thames & Hudson, 2000, p. 219.

identified. Simonides, however, was able to recall by memory the seating order and thus the bodies of the deceased could be buried with dignity by members of their families and so Ars memoriae was born.[21]

This MSC event passed down to us by Simonides suggests that architectural total destruction has very little to do with "the destruction of memory".[22] The local storage effect of episodic functions of the memory works most effectively when the location in question has collapsed. One only has to look at the debate going on about Berlin's castle to find confirmation of this: The buildings, which crave our attention the most, collapsed, with a great deal of noise and causing much sympathy. 'Ex-architecture' is the most steadfast neuronally speaking of all types of architecture.

The question arises, is there a calculated memoactive architecture which is not destructive and which operates on a lower level of imprinting but all the same has consequences? Is there a transmission potential which can be applied as a *constructive* architectonic practice? If ex-architecture constitutes the ultimate of a success in enculturation, what follows then in a fictive scale of memoactivity in the next locations?

There are 'exit-architectures' which take up position directly behind ex-architectures. Escape routes and emergency exits are in fact anti-stress architectures which constantly remind us of the worst case thus demolishing any thoughts of a safe and secure interior.

---

[21] Cf. Cicero: *De oratore, II*, published 55 BC.
[22] Already the title indicates Robert Bevan's unconvincing message that destroyed architecture means destroyed memory: *The Destruction of Memory: Architecture at War*, London: Reaktion Books, 2006.

Standing buildings firstly enculturate when there is a population of users which are put under stress by the architecture, for example when it is too confined, and secondly when the majority of this population can, in a positive sense, come to terms with this stress as in "We were there and we survived". Both prerequisites apply to the House of Commons in London. When there are important decisions to be made it is hopelessly overcrowded and a perspiratory collective is the result. The side effects of such buildings are feelings of claustrophobia and impulse to flight etc.

„*We shape our buildings, and afterwards our buildings shape us.*" Churchill's compliment to the energies of construction was therefore poisoned. It meant uncomfortable and demanding houses. His conclusions correspond to the awkward message which mnemonics directs at architects: A building is a success if one can save oneself from it.

2. Entry/Exit

It is customary to limit the potential for making an impression to the surface of an architecture. But buildings are not only faces but also landscapes.[23] Not only do they consist of façades but also routes, and it is the latter which support observations of architecture from the approach of transmission theory. Architectonic transmission is inconceivable without the method of *hodos* – of the way. It is no coincidence that Kurt Lewin, who conceived the science of hodology – of marked out routes in a topological structure –, was much influenced by the First

---

[23]   Cf. Gilles Deleuze and Félix Guattari: *Tausend Plateaus* (1980), Berlin: Merve, 1992, p. 229.

World War.[24] The front is the starting point of the most emotionally saturated of all routes: On the way home relaxation spreads among the troops – with some definitely very architectonic consequences as evident in the tradition of triumphal arches and other 'entry-architectures'.

Among all contemporary architectural codifications it is not the entry- but much more the exit-regulations which influence construction enduringly. It would be an exaggeration to claim that the latter enjoy considerable esteem among architects. But every complex construction project starts with the planning of escape routes; before the design of skyscraper comes the design of escape from the skyscraper. Notwithstanding professional designers are well-known for preferring to speak of 'entry situations' rather than 'exit situations'. Architects belong to an entry-fixated profession which, by means of the architectural means available, is always trying to say "Welcome!". They are still enthralled by the idea of an occupational image of building houses as being equivalent to creating homeland. It was not until the catastrophe of 9/11 and the competition for Ground Zero that there has been a gradual valorisation of exit spaces. Since with these events discussion started to take place for the first time in the history of architecture about escape routes of new building projects, not only in the form of isolated circles of experts but also a wide and enervated public. Ever since, the well-meant question of all designers, how one can best enter a building is accompanied by a subtle anachronistic undercurrent which even architectural novices will not fail to perceive.

What is the best way to leave architecture behind you? This is now the question.

---

[24] Cf. Kurt Lewin: "Kriegslandschaft" (1917), in: Jörg Dünne and Stephan Günzel (eds.): *Raumtheorie: Grundlagentexte aus Philosophie und Kulturwissenschaften*, Frankfurt am Main: Suhrkamp, 2006, p. 129.

2.1 Hubris and *decorum*

Populations are influenced more by higher rather than lower intensities of stress. The relaxation phase after an MSC event is considered the most important donor of cultural order. The decisive question is in which condition does a population relax: Does a positive or negative stress evaluation take place? Does one feel oneself the winner or the loser?

The struggle for a good ranking for one of the opponents can end in three ways, with dominance, subdominance (stalemate) or submission. Physiology knows that only dominance makes the one subjected to stress physically healthier than before. Subdominance and submission will eventually lead to physical damage. While the first one may result in heart and circulatory damage of both parties – the heightened general alertness demands its tribute – the total defeat of the last one often ends in a stomach ulcer.

Not only physiological stress of the individual can be discerned but also the effects of stress culturally have become evident. In Western culture they are reflected in the multifarious codifications also architectonically.

We can distinguish between two kinds of architectural codification: building codes* and design codes*. Both attempt to keep possible dangers and risks under control. Design codes are there to prevent the threat of a design, with which the presumed public has no comprehension (and control the architectural appearance, proportions, façades and materials used); building codes are there to guarantee for the stability of the building and in the case of fire to ensure the survival of the users of the building (and control the minimum width of escape routes and their maximum length).[25] Edward Mitchell regards codification as a formation of knowledge which constructively processes irritating events: "... codes are a means of taking events – unpredictable, chaotic singularities – and representing them as knowledge."[26] This way of seeing things fits well to Pierre Bourdieu's definition of codification as the practise of safety: "As a general tendency one could formulate that the practice tends to be more strongly codified depending on how dangerous the situation is. ... Codification means making safe at the same time as giving form." [27]

Architectural codification has always deactivated security issues based on if-then-rules, however the *forms* of deactivation have always been subject to big changes. As a basic principle it can be said that the adjustment of the visual appearance of architecture precedes any considerations as to the safety of a building. Design codes are older than building codes – the latter didn't become commonplace until the 18th and 19th centuries.[28]

Especially in the case of the Romans, design codes can be found which proved to be of subsequent significance and influenced building centuries later. For instance the Emperor Domitian decreed a law pertaining to the alignment of buildings which,

* English terms also in the German original [translator's note].

[25] Cf. Edward Mitchell: "Fear Factors", in: *Perspecta 35: Building Codes*, Cambridge, Mass.: The MIT Press, 2004, p. 144.

[26] Ibid.

[27] Pierre Bourdieu: "Kode und Kodifizierung", in: Johanna Hofbauer, Gerald Prabitz and Josef Wallmannsberger (eds.): *Bilder, Symbole, Metaphern. Visualisierung und Informierung in der Moderne*, Vienna: Passagen, 1998, pp. 225-226.

[28] The first *building code* is generally considered to be a passage from the Babylonian codex of Hammurabi (18th century B.C.), although this does not refer to the safety of the building but rather the liability of the builder. "'If a builder constructs a building for a citizen and fails to carry this out properly resulting in the house which he has built collapsing and thus killing the occupant, then the builder is to be killed." – Cf. Hans-Dieter Viel: *Der Codex Hammurapi*, Göttingen: Duehrkohp + Radicke, 2002.

as a result of Justinian legislation, survived well into the Middle Ages. Evidence for it can still be found in Strasbourg's oldest municipal law from the 12th century.[29] "Wherever persons of authority – be it king, prince or city parliament – appeared as a creator of standardizations in regard to building construction, this occurred on the one hand under aesthetic considerations as to beautification of the surroundings and on the other hand as an expression of centralized power."[30]

The rules of *decorum* can be considered the most important pre-modern design codes.[31] Here we are dealing with a multimedia ranking system which emerged from the rhetoric of antiquity and taught commensurateness and accuracy: "Language and subject matter should be harmonized with each other, a sublime theme requires a sublime style and an unostentatious theme an unostentatious style."[32] The sublime means in this case sharing those effects involving collective insurance of existence, i.e. sink or swim for the population.[33] By the time of Horace the rules of *decorum* had already passed to poetry and the fine arts, by the time of Vitruvius to architecture as well.

In the danger orientated war culture of the Imperium Romanum the entire society and its artefacts were subject to *decorum*. The ranking of a building within the *decorum* spectrum could be seen from its *ornamentum*. The *ornamentum* relates to the *decorum* like the individual note to the piano keyboard. The highest

---

29 Klaus Jan Philipp: "Normierung 'avant la lettre'. Eine Blütenlese", in: Walter Prigge (ed.): *Ernst Neufert – Normierte Baukultur*, Frankfurt am Main: Campus, 1999, p. 300.

30 Ibid.

31 Cf. Mühlmann, *The Nature of Cultures*, pp. 46-47.

32 Gérard Raulet: "Ornament", in: *Historisches Wörterbuch der Rhetorik*, ed. by Gert Ueding, Tübingen: Max Niemeyer, 2003, p. 425.

33 Cf. Heiner Mühlmann: *Ästhetische Theorie der Renaissance. Leon Battista Alberti*, Bochum: Marcel Dolega, ²2005, p. 169.

ornamentum was reserved for those buildings which contributed the most to success in war, the temples where the gods condescended to be merciful. By spanning the two extremes of 'sublime' and 'low' *decorum* formed a consistent codification system relating to war: "The ranking obtains its characteristics from the defining of the whole by war, i.e. the sublime. It expresses: closest to war, second closest to war etc."[34] The reason that the city wall remained more or less without decoration but at the same time was considered high architecture was because it formed the basis for the entire *decorum* spectrum. By protecting a population by means of its fortifications, it was the city wall which made a system of decoration ranking at all possible in the first place.

If the temple – protected by the city wall – can be regarded as antiquity's most important piece of stress architecture, then the triumphal arch must be its central relaxation architecture. Triumphal arches are 'the-day-after' constructions. The battle has been won and a spectacular entry into the city is prepared for the triumphant general. The triumphal arch is not a gate, it only represents one,[35] it is an entry-hypostasis. The purpose of the *arci triumphalis*, of which alone in Rome 36 have been counted, was solely for the transmission of information and the immortalization of the days' events.[36]

The triumphal arch was not only the gateway for the returning army, it also constituted the eye of the needle for the transmission of *decorum* in the extensive symbolic space of West-

---

[34] Mühlmann, *The Nature of Cultures*, p. 119.
[35] Cf. Mühlmann, *The Nature of Cultures*, p. 51.
[36] Cf. Wolfgang Pehnt: "Drinnen und draußen: Splitter und Späne zur Geschichte der Tür", in: Otl Aicher, Jürgen Becker and Wolfgang Pehnt (eds.): *Zugänge – Ausgänge*, photos by Timm Rautert, Cologne: Verlag der Buchhandlung Walther König, 1990, p. 8.

ern classical architecture. It was the triumphal arch which appeared by means of *ornamentum* in the Italian city states of the Renaissance striving for Roman greatness. In 1470, as Alberti designed the façade for the Church of San Andrea in Mantua modelled on the Severus Arch, the triumphal arch itself ended up in its own dynamics of transmission [Figs. 2, 9]. A process started which could be termed 'general architectural downsizing'. Suddenly bonsai triumphal arches were being projected onto façades, door frames, fire places etc. – not only had the *ornamentum* but also the shrunken forms of triumphal monuments become transmission units.

Why though did *decorum* disappear little by little in the 17th, 18th and 19th centuries? What led to the relativization of the classical and its obligatory ornamentation? And why did the entry-paradigm vanish into thin air?

If the buildings on the Acropolis or the architecture of Forum Romanum had been suspected of being isolated freestanding constructions, with the 'user interfaces' mounted on pillars, which became widespread in absolutistic France, any contradictions that appeared were not between individual buildings but between the temple-like façades and the body of the building behind it. Complete streets, squares and areas of a city got a classical upgrading.[37] It was as if the temple's main trait, the sacred interior called the *temenos*, had moved to the urban exterior, as if urbanity had been burdened with being responsible for success in war, appeasing the Gods and for a better world in general. And as if in doing this one had forgotten to create new quasi-divine dimensional references.

---

[37]   Cf. Alexander Tzonis and Liane Lefaivre: *Das Klassische in der Architektur. Die Poetik der Ordnung*, Bauwelt Fundamente 72, Braunschweig: Vieweg, 1987, p. 198.

Fig. 2: The triumph of the triumphal arch: Leon Battista Alberti's
S. Andrea in Mantua, constructed in 1470.

But one new architectonic dimensional reference did indeed
arise in the France of the 17th and 18th centuries – the human
being, or to be more precise: the human being observed as an
observer. In doing this the individual – and not the population
represented by a general – reclaimed the vacant position of a
dimensional reference to rule adjustments. The cradle of the
observed observer was ensured at a safe distance by a front
which defined an extensive space of relaxation. Only by means
of widespread territorial pacification, brought about by the formation of the modern nations, could taste in the 17th century,
and aesthetics as an independent philosophical discipline in

the 18th century arise. The reason why the national boundaries, as potential demarcation lines between war and peace, gradually shifted into the shadows is obvious: military superiority. This superiority is due to the ballistic innovations i.e. artillery – the 'war of the engineers' which has its roots in the 18th and 19th centuries.

From then on, the most technically advanced engineers had the safeguarding of borders in their sights while the architects mainly had the peaceful interior of the state's territory in theirs. By the 16th century the construction of fortifications had become an area for specialists and by the early 17th century differences can be found between the engineer responsible for the *architectura militaris* and the architect entirely devoted to *architectura civilis*.[38] Until the beginning of the 18th century however, both forms of architecture were under the auspices of one person fulfilling both the role of master builder and engineer, but at the end of this century war culture was divided: war and culture went their separate ways.

And with that the death knell of *decorum* was sounded. Those who are able to wage war competently and professionally, do not have to remember their victory culturally. *Decorum* had been vanquished by outstanding bellicose fitness. The signs of dominion can be found almost everywhere on the earth's surface and this is reflected in the unadorned surfaces of Western architecture. "The face of cultural power, which causes this hubris, is not the face of the triumphant warrior but the face of the innocent artist and philosopher. The culture which has subdued everything is inside innocent and unsuspecting."[39]

---

[38] Cf. Hartwig Neumann: *Festungsbaukunst und Festungsbautechnik. Deutsche Wehrbauarchitektur vom XV. bis XX. Jahrhundert*, Koblenz: Bernard & Graefe, 1988, p. 142.

[39] Mühlmann, *The Nature of Cultures*, p. 115.

But what is wrong with paradise? What is so bad about cultural ignorance of the fact that Western transcendental humanistic modernity has forgotten its own aggression by means of its successful military apparatus? The problem is a phenomenon, known as the Baldwin effect in evolutionary biology, the cultural analytical applicability of which has recently become much less contested.[40]

The Baldwin effect describes relationships between ontogenetic learning and phylogenetic instinctive behaviour. In contrast to Lamarckism it does not deal with the *direct* transition of that which has been acquired in the genes of an *individual*, but rather with the *indirect* heredity transmission of that which has been acquired in a *population*. Baldwin's theory says among other things that genetically generated capabilities for innovative learning might be favoured by evolution so that the combination of organic traits (learning ability) and capabilities learned ontogenetically increase reproductive fitness.

But the Baldwin effect also harbours dangers. It is possible, that the learning successes achieved by inherited learning ability only have to be imitated thus enabling a life that is carefree. Then the pressure of selection, which influences the genetically provided apparatus of the innovative learning ability, vanishes, and evolutionary theory speaks of 'shielding' of the genetic apparatus from selective pressure. It is possible that the genetically generated learning ability disappears unnoticed from the gene pool under such shielded conditions.

Decorum disappeared under such shielded conditions: The cultural warring allusion evaporated at the point where wars

[40] Cf. Bruce H. Weber and David J. Depew (eds.): *Evolution and Learning: The Baldwin Effect Reconsidered*, Cambridge, Mass.: The MIT Press, 2003.

33

had become a walk-over for the superior forces. Thus in Holland in the 17th century *decorum* was bid farewell without much ado: "Colonial trade and skilled defence against other powers facilitated physical survival, the precondition for shielding effect and goal regression."[41] For instance the genre of Dutch interior painting, which manages to do without the traditional *decorum* rules, could only arise in an age which described itself as 'golden'.

The Baldwin effect can be a mixed blessing. It rewards those who are only required to make an imitatory effort at learning with a lightness of being. On the other hand it succeeds in damaging the primary, genetically transferred instrument of learning ability, the cognitive apparatus. The cultural population continues to live as comfortably as ever since the imitative behaviour is as successful as before. When however a change in the surroundings occurs thus resulting in the ineffectiveness of the imitative behaviour, everything must be learnt again, starting from scratch, innovatively. And if there is only inadequate learning ability available then the results are catastrophic: A process of annihilation begins. The Baldwin effect means: A population forgets how to learn because it is no longer required for life or survival.

The rise of modernity has transported the observed observer into the centre of its attention but he has been since then to much involved in himself and its humanism than to be able to recognize the most important thing i.e. the aggressive hubris of his own culture and its technologically created advantages in the struggle for life. The relocation of truth in the eye of the beholder has resulted in a cultural self-deception of the West, of its own benevolence. "The Western individual can neither

---

[41] Mühlmann, *The Nature of Cultures*, p. 109.

imagine that his culture would be capable of humiliating or destroying another culture nor can he imagine his own culture being humiliated or destroyed by another. Other cultures do not share this complacency."[42] The threat of the Baldwin effect is especially relevant at the present time.

2.2 Shock Corridors

Between the 15th and 17th centuries the state took charge of all matters pertaining to warfare by monopolizing all weapons which would be of any use in the case of an emergency and by setting up organized supply chains. The days when soldiers had to equip themselves and private warlords were a thing of the past and an epoch of modern nationalized warfare could begin. "The territorial state guaranteed peace within and claimed for itself the exclusive right to issue a declaration of war; this was achieved by the art of separating interior and exterior, friend or foe, war and peace etc."[43]

Does a paradigmatic space of modernity which can be considered a kind of architectonic guarantee for internal stability exist?

It does and it is called 'corridor'. The corridor is the unplanned result of a contemporary Western state which projects its ubiquitous power onto its interior which has to be placated. The fact that the corridor is a by-product of nationalized warfare is paralleled by the fascinating history of its terminology. In the 14th

---

[42] Mühlmann, *The Nature of Cultures*, p. 115.
[43] Herfried Münkler: *Über den Krieg: Stationen der Kriegsgeschichte im Spiegel ihrer theoretischen Reflexion*, Weilerswist: Velbrück, [2]2005, p. 224.

century the old Italian term *corridóre*, derived from the Latin *currere* (to run) referred to a way on top of fortification walls. It was not until the 19th century that *corridóre* turned into *corridóio* meaning a way *inside* a building and then in the 20th century reversed back to describing an external environment ('Polish corridor'). This movement of terminology – from the outside to the inside and to the outside again – does not only apply to Italian but is also to be found correspondingly in French, English and German. In all these languages the 'corridor' started its career as a term in the building of fortifications and as a fortified dividing line between the city and the wilderness, then in the course of the following centuries found its way into almost all non-bellicose architectural structures of the territorial state and finally ended up being exteriorized in the first third of the 20th century and becoming a term with a decidedly military ring to it as in 'peace corridor'.

The first cannons which appeared in the 15th century revolutionized the architecture of fortifications. The defensive walls became lower and thicker.[44] Henceforth attackers no longer tried to scale the walls using ladders but to breach them. This transformation began in Italy which was devastated by Charles VIII's campaigns. The French had revolutionary weapons with explosive force in tow, cast bronze cannons armed with iron cannonballs. The defenders reacted with the so-called 'trace italienne', a new kind of fortification system which depended on multiangular bastions leaving no blind spots [Fig. 3].

In the process the corridor plummeted from the top to the bottom, from the walkways *above* off *into* the ditches next to the fortifying walls. The corridor became known as the 'covered way'. Its inven-

---

[44]   Cf. Hubertus Günther: "Die Kriegskunst in der Renaissance", in: Hubertus Günther (ed.): *Deutsche Architekturtheorie zwischen Gotik und Renaissance*, Darmstadt: Wissenschaftliche Buchgesellschaft, 1988, p. 167.

tor is said to be Niccolò Tartaglia. "In 1556 Tartaglia made the excellent suggestion of stationing some of the infantry in a walkway (*via coperta* or *via segreta*) which was to be cut into the top of the counter rim of the ditch."[45] As of the 17th century the walkway between ditch and glacis was seldom called a corridor with the result that Johann Gottfried von Hoyer wrote quite rightly in 1818: "*Corridor* is the old name for the covered way which is no longer used today, it now applies to connecting ways in barracks, armouries etc. when a number of rooms are connected."[46]

While the corridor in the *architectura militaris* of the Age of Enlightenment was marginalized as a term, in the *architectura civilis* it pervaded spatially and terminologically all the more. Especially in modern social spheres did it find increasing acceptance. Dominion in a society that had become 'bourgeois' objectified itself above all in the corridors of asylums and prisons. Architecture was decreasingly codified by rules of *decorum* but more through typologies. Methods of classification inspired by zoology started to take hold. "Following this analogy, those whose task it was to design the new types of public and private buildings ... began to talk of the plan and sectional distribution in the same terms as the constitutional organization of species; axes and vertebrae became virtually synonymous."[47]

While the corridor passed through nearly all modern typologies of the architectura civilis, a fundamental displacement of architectonic principles was associated with this. While the pre-modern age was dominated by the principle of passing through (city gate,

---

[45] Christopher Duffy: *Siege Warfare: The Fortress in the Early Modern World 1494-1660*, London/New York: Routledge, 1979, p. 34.

[46] Johann Gottfried von Hoyer: *Allgemeines Wörterbuch der Kriegsbaukunst*, 3 Vol., Berlin: 1817-18.

[47] Anthony Vidler: "The Third Typology" (1977), in: K. Michael Hays (ed.): *Architecture Theory since 1968*, Cambridge, Mass./London: The MIT Press, 1998, p. 289.

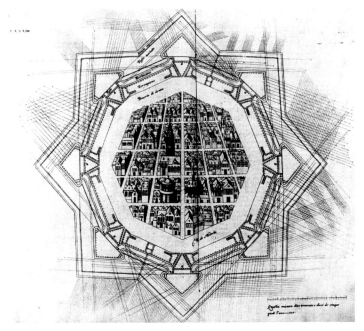

Fig. 3: Construction of fortifications without blind spots: The *trace italienne* in a design by Francesco de Marchi, 1599.

triumphal arch, enfilade etc.) the modern age gave way to the principle of passing by. The rooms with many doors gave way to the rooms with the one door, the transversal gave way to the tangential. Robin Evans linked this process with the development of a compensatory illusory freedom of the eye which is accompanied by an all the more persistent dependency of the body and soul: "As the room closed in, so the aesthetic of space unfolded, as if the extensive liberty of the eye were a consolation for the closer confinement of body and soul", writes Evans about the architecture of Sir John Soane – "a form of compensation which was to become more familiar and more pronounced in 20th century architecture".[48]

---

[48] Robin Evans: "Figures, Doors, Passages" (1978), in: Robin Evans: *Translations from Drawing to Building and Other Essays*, London: AA Publications, 1997, p. 76.

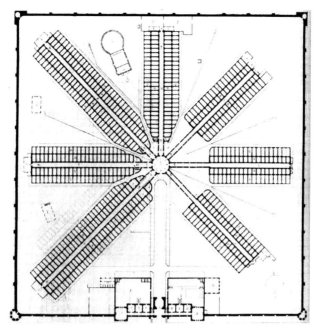

Fig. 4: Panoptic corridors: John Haviland's Eastern State Penitentiary, Philadelphia, 1829.

The end of the 18th century witnessed the first larger prisons in which the principle of the rows of monks cells were reflected. Communal dungeons were now a thing of the past. Ghent's Maison de Force built in 1772 exhibits four rows of cells accessed via colonnades. Although the arrangement of rooms suffered from complexity, 50 years later such problems had been removed. In the radial plan prisons, which appeared in the first third of 19th century, the centre of the building was transformed from an enclosed courtyard as was the case in the Maison de Force to an all-controlling surveillance nerve centre. The influence of Jeremy Bentham's Panopticon is unmistakable. Why this was a landmark in the history of prison architecture but nevertheless proved to be not 'fit' enough to be transmitted to the next generation is exemplified by two penitentiaries built in Pennsylvania. The Western State Penitentiary in Allegheny County built in 1826 as panopticon turned out to be a security risk because the circular periphery had been designed too large. The facility had to be demolished after only seven years. The Eastern State Penitentiary however, finished in 1829 and still in operation until 1971, was more economically organized as only the corridors and not the cells could be viewed from the central surveillance personnel [Fig. 4].

In hospital planning in recent times the corridor has also been able to establish itself although not at the same speed everywhere. Michel Foucault has described the 'consideration of the openings' as follows. "It must facilitate the observation of the patients and the coordination of their care; the design of the building must prevent infection by means of effective isolation; the air circulating round each bed must prevent a stagnation of any noxious vapours which might have a harmful effect on the patient's fluids and worsen the disease."[49] Pioneers in the building of hospitals with corridors were to be found especially in the German speaking world where the tendency has been since the 19th century to scale down the size of the wards and to make the interconnected departments more specialized. The Katharinenhospital in Stuttgart built by Nikolaus von Thouret in 1817 consists of three wings connected by corridors. The municipal hospital in Dresden designed by Theodor Friedrich 1817-1874 follows this principle of corridors too.

The 19th century can be seen as the century of the corridor. Suddenly the corridor was to be found everywhere in asylums and administrative buildings, in the country homes and urban

---

[49]   Michel Foucault: *Überwachen und Strafen. Die Geburt des Gefängnisses*, Frankfurt am Main: Suhrkamp, 1976, p. 223.

apartments of the middle classes and in the high-rise blocks of the industrial age. Only its bad reputation could outrival its proliferation. How could such and unpopular room become so omnipresent?

The transmission theory explains cultural evolution irrespective of sympathy addresses. Buildings enculturate, it was said, only if a building causes stress while at the same time remaining under the trauma threshold and when the majority of re-exit-beings can celebrate properly. Both points apply to the 'enclosure-milieu' of prisons etc. With Foucault's notion of 'discipline' it is appropriate to speak of 'disciplinary enculturation' since the going past (by wardens, doctors etc.) precedes the going out (ex-criminals, ex-inmates, ex-patients etc.). Anybody discharged into the inner 'outside' of the territorial state was considered 'normal'. This is the way 'total institutions' created the central enculturation archipelagos which were able to influence the entire country with their disciplinary measures. Unlike the *decorum* epoch which brought about an 'enculturation from above', modern institutions provided an 'enculturation from below'. The delinquent was enculturated before the good citizen, the insane before the sane, the sick before the healthy. The institution's corridors served as the territory where comparisons were drawn. It was there that the evaluating look established itself registering the differences between individual cell inmates to transfer them to a regime of normality. One day, says Foucault, it will be possible to show how "the relationships in the family, above all in the parent/child 'cell', have 'disciplined' since classical times by adopting external models stemming from school, military, and then medicine, psychiatry and psychology".[50]

---

[50] Foucault, *Überwachen und Strafen*, p. 277.

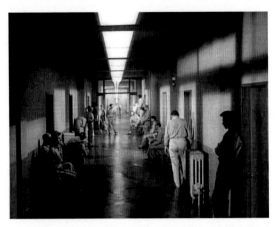

Fig. 5: Disciplinary enculturation: Scene from the film *Shock Corridor*, directed by Samuel Fuller, 1963.

As Samuel Fuller in 1963 made his film *Shock Corridor*, not only had the corridor ended up in the most remote corner of the architectural environment but also had become a geopolitically connoted metaphor. The film tells the story of an ambitious journalist Johnny Barrett who in order to win the Pulitzer Prize hatches a daring plan to masquerade as a sexual deviant in order to gain access to a mental hospital, to mingle with the patients and crack an unsolved murder case and write a prize-winning story. Barrett succeeds having himself committed 'undercover' but things take a turn for the worse: He becomes mentally disordered. Much of the plot takes place in the hospital's corridor, which is significantly called 'Main Street' by the personnel. In this corridor Fuller presents the American unconsciousness. Slap bang in the middle of the Camelot Era of US history – those confident, youthful days before Kennedy's assassination and the Vietnam War – the Afro-American campaigns for the Cu Clux Clan, the soldier fights the wars of past days and the atomic physicist degenerates into infantility. The climax of the film is one of the most memorable in the his-

Fig. 6: Beyond inner and outer: Scene from *Shock Corridor*.

tory of cinema: Suddenly it begins to rain in the corridor, there is lightning. Soaking wet Barrett runs from one closed door to the next. Main Street, it appears, does not offer a way out anymore because the border(line) between sane and pathological no longer coincides with inner and outer space in the hospital [Figs. 5, 6].

2.3 Paranoiac Chreodology

Modern enclosure-milieus such as the prison, the hospital and the factory have been facing a deep crisis since the 20th century. In the place of disciplinary enculturation appeared those seemingly liberal evaluations, which one could, in the style of Gilles Deleuze, term as 'controlling' enculturation. "In a disciplinary society one never stops starting something (from the school to the barracks, and from the barracks to the factory), whereas in the controlling society one never finishes anything. Businesses, further education and services are metastable and co-existing states of one and the same modulation which resembles a universal distorter."[51] Entire institutions are diffusing more and more in their environments, ubiquitous and pervasive structures are becoming more common. The US-American criminal judiciary has developed alternatives to prisons in the shape of 'electronic foot chains' which are presently in use on approximately 100,000 people, similarly numerous factories in the Western world have been transformed into gaseous entities in which uninterrupted 'self-techniques' have superseded the old certainties in regard to class and wages.

The 20th century put disciplinary society in perspective but not the corridor. The latter continued to prove itself useful, even when functionalism and new styles in construction branded it as 'bad architecture'.[52] Why was the corridor not banished into oblivion at the time when disciplinary society gave way to control society? Why didn't a Baldwin effect strike at the moment when acquired knowledge had been rendered soft, indeed imperceptible by regimes of normality?

It should be said from the start that the somnolence of the 'Baldwinized' modern age was always accompanied by a paranoiac relentless vigilance, and it is this vigilance which found a use for then corridor in post-modern times. At the moment when control succeeded discipline, the corridor was reborn as a compulsory emergency exit required by law – 'Corridor 2.0'.

---

[51]   Gilles Deleuze: "Postskriptum über die Kontrollgesellschaften", in: Gilles Deleuze: *Unterhandlungen 1972-1990*, Frankfurt am Main: Suhrkamp, 1990, p. 257.

[52]   Le Corbusier especially turned out to be a veritable hater of corridors – at least in his rhetoric. "Out of streets of corridors became cities of corridors", he complained, "The entire city consists of corridors. What a sight! What happened to aesthetics? We say nothing – we suffer. How quickly we are satisfied! What would you think of an architect who presented you the plans of a house which consisted of nothing but corridors?" – Cf. Le Corbusier: *1929 – Feststellungen zu Architektur und Städtebau*, Bauwelt Fundamente 12, Braunschweig/Wiesbaden: Vieweg, 1987, pp. 159-160.

Fig. 7: Exit-Chreode: "Fluchtweg" by Alena Meier, GASAG-Haus, Berlin, 1995.

Ways that are necessary have a name: 'chreodes' (from the Greek *chré* 'must', and *hodos* 'way'). The chreode of Corridor 2.0 is a novelty in the architectural evolution as in a spectacular reversal of the premodern entry fixation it involves the fastest possible exit from the building. Escape routes are ways home but rotated by 180 degrees. *Decorum* marked the happy end for successful warriors returning home whereas the exit codifications point the way to 'freedom'.* The fact that this 'freedom' is merely a relative freedom of control society is an indication of the success of its transmission [Fig. 7].

Between the design codes of *decorum* and the building codes of escape route codifications stands a modern age which has been able to substitute dangers with risks.[53] Initially it was the mid-

---

* In the German original the term "Das Freie" not only means "freedom" but also unroofed environment [translator's note].

[53] Cf. Wolfgang Bonß: *Vom Risiko: Unsicherheit und Ungewißheit in der Moderne*, Hamburg: Hamburger Edition, 1995; also Niklas Luhmann: *Soziologie des Risikos*, Berlin/New York: de Gruyter, 2003.

dle-class merchants of early capitalism in Italy who, in a dare-devil manner, substituted the Roman topos of Fortuna i.e. the unfathomable resolution of the Gods by voluntarily undertaking perilous voyages known as *avienture*. Whosoever undertook such risks, as these people did, for them the future was not a reproduction of a never-ending cosmological order but rather the result of independent action. While danger is accompanied by superstitious strategies to guarantee safety, in the case of risk a calculating approach towards uncertainty is evident. Dangers are independent of a subject whereas risks assume a subject which gives a vote of no confidence.

The more uncertainties constitute risks, the more the rise of the insurance sector becomes apparent. The origins of which, it will be no surprise to discover, are to be found in trade in the 15th century. Somewhat later at the end of the 17th century fire insurances meant that it was the turn of households. Thus in 1676 in Hamburg the first institution for the insurance of buildings – the General-Feuer-Cassa – was founded. The insurance industry really became firmly established between 1700 and 1850: "In this stage insurance arose as a viable system applicable to numerous uncertainties."[54] Above all the principle of insuring persons and property began to spread at this time; something that would have been inconceivable before the Reformation. With the expansion of the insurance industry as of 1850 insurance became the standard mode in dealing with uncertainty and increasingly concentrated on dealing not only with individual but also social risk.[55] Finally by around 1900 the state was able to get in on the act and become the largest insurance institution of all.

---

[54] Bonß, *Vom Risiko*, p. 180.
[55] Ibid.

The risk-oriented modern age, in which the insurance industry so cleverly became established as a key element, marginalized *decorum*. Design codes nonetheless continued to play a certain role (as they still do today) but it was the building codes which were to prove to have the greater impact. As early as the beginning of the 19th century the US metropolis began to introduce construction guidelines and the first law requiring the inspection of public places and public buildings was passed in New Orleans in 1865. One thing that prompted the need for action by state and community in matters of standardization were the catastrophes which occurred in the increasingly crowded cities. A promise by the state of future security is always born in the aftermath of a disaster. The Great Fire of Chicago of 1871 acted last but not least as a catalyst for the development of many new building codes which are generally debated in standardization committees created by the state and where representatives of insurance companies are in attendance.

Design codes like building codes not only unify the lack of authorship but also the relationship to stress. The former materialize in the relaxation phase after the triumph, the latter traditionally arise after catastrophes, fires and the collapsing of buildings etc. In contrast to design codes, building codes dispense with any form of positive stress evaluation however. Their answer to the stress event cannot be termed vainglorious dominance but rather prudent subdominance. While the *decorum* rule adjustment forms a codification after the disaster, building codes are the formation of order prior to the disaster (nonetheless they emanate from coping with previous troubles). They are the results of civilisation i.e. the products of a technical, judicial and political evolution by employing self-enthrallment.[56] Only a 'state of emergency' can break through the coherence of the legal framework. It was described as "accepting the external into the law".[57] Major and minor catastrophes which shape the murky foundations of building codes represent nothing other than that. If the person who must make decisions relating to a state of emergency is sovereign, then that which is sovereign in modern architectural codification must be the case of damage or loss.

Escape routes are as old as architecture itself – one only has to think of the secret escape routes from castles in antiquity and the Middle Ages, for example the Passetto di Borgo, an 800-meter long passage which Pope Nicholas III had constructed in 1277 to enable his escape from the Vatican to Castle St. Angelo in times of crisis. However, it was not until the 20th century that compulsory escape routes were required by law. As far back as in 1878 Anna Connelly registered her patent for a fire escape, a system of steel staircases affixed to the façades of multi-storeyed buildings, but it was not until after 1900 that it found its way into the building codes of American cities [Fig. 8]. Nowadays it is not vertical but horizontal routes which must be regarded as exit architecture par excellence. It is primarily in the chreodes which lead to the staircase and for reasons of cost and safety more often than not take the form a corridor, that we can find the exit sign generally used internationally.

German building regulations fall under the jurisdiction of the individual federal states but by means of model building code (*Musterbauordnung*, MBO) it has become relatively uniform throughout the country and by using the term 'Rettungsweg'

---

[56] On "self-enthrallment as *decorum* of the modern age" see Mühlmann, *Kunst und Krieg*, 1998.

[57] Giorgio Agamben: *Homo sacer. Die souveräne Macht und das nackte Leben*, Frankfurt am Main: Suhrkamp, 2002, p. 43.

Fig. 8: Façade as Exit-Architecture: A typical fire escape, New York.

rescue route has combined two aims, firstly to allow fire fighters etc. access to the building to save life in the case of fire but also so that people can save themselves and escape. On the basis of these two aims as defined above, the building codes in Germany have precise requirements as to the number and character of the rescue routes. Paragraphs 34 to 36 of the MBO mention 'staircases necessary', 'essential stairwell space' and 'corridors necessary'. Through them runs the so-called 'first' i.e. structural rescue route. The MBO requires two 'Rettungswege' independent of each other for each user (e.g. apartment, shop, practice etc.) with rooms (by rooms are meant those that are not for temporary use). By 'independent of each other' is meant that should the first rescue route become dysfunctional, this will have no effect on the functionality of the second exit route. The first rescue route for storeys other than the ground floor must run via the essential stairs, the second rescue route may run via the fire brigades special rescue equipment such as ladders, hydraulic platforms and turntable fire-escapes.

Architectonic chreodes will be investigated by 'chreodology' which has yet to be defined precisely. What can be said for certain is that panic research, which has in recent years become a digitally supported multi-particle system, will have contributed much to our understanding of chreodology. The latest panic simulations describe crowds of people as self-organized multi-particle systems consisting of individual particles weighing 80kg, with variable width of shoulders, having a target velocity and a definite force of repulsion to other individuals as well as a so-called 'panic factor'. The more nervous the individual becomes, the weaker is his ability to critically assess the movements of the crowd and to choose the best possible outcome.[58] Constructionally speaking the so-called 'panic column' is one of the most important findings of panic research. This column is placed like a wave break in front of emergency exits. Surveys have shown that panic columns are most effective when placed not in the middle but slightly off-centre. Cushioned, embellished or illuminated they are becoming increasingly used in stadiums, airports and office buildings.

Above all chreodes are to be found where architecture is a matter of life or death, rescue routes and victory architecture. While the pre-modern age codified its entry chreodes by means of *decorum*, the present age regulates its exit chreodes by means of building codes. The enculturating events behind *decorum* was

---

[58] Dirk Helbing, Ilés Farkas and Tamás Vicsek: "Simulating dynamical features of escape panic", in: *Nature*, Vol. 407, 28. September 2000, pp. 487-490.

the unforgettable marching in of the victorious army. Laurel wreathes and the like were soon to be transformed into stone architectural decoration. Nowadays the triumphant procession has been superseded by a systemic processing of disasters and sporadic evacuation drills which serve to remind the users of buildings that not everything which functions everyday is safe.

The dynamics of transmission of *decorum* and building codes could not be more different. While the transmission of *decorum* is passed on culturally (above all based on Roman successes still reverberating in the Renaissance), the transmission of building codes relies on civilisatory dissemination of laws, norms and guidelines. The enculturating event is in both cases the same, i.e. destroyed architecture. Only for one small difference, the ex-architecture of *decorum* belonged to the opponents in war, whereas the ex-architecture of the building codes belongs to one's own population. *Tempi passati*: That which was the triumphal arch of the pre-modern age is now the panic column of the present age, and the only contemporary essential decoration which architecture has at its disposal is the 'exit sign' [Figs. 9, 10].

When Vincent Mazeau in 2003 modified an exit sign with the word 'EVIL' and fixed it on the wall of an emergency corridor in a theatre this was much more than just a warning to leave the building [Fig. 11]. And not just for the reason that it was art. 'EXIT/EVIL' posed the vexing question about the relationships between architecture and paranoia.

Paranoia is a chronic psychosis which is characterized by a more or less systemized delusion, the predominance of interpretation and the lack of reduction in intelligence.[59] It can be

---

[59] Cf. Jean Laplanche and Jean-Bertrand Pontalis: *Das Vokabular der Psychoanalyse*, Vol. 2, Frankfurt am Main: Suhrkamp, 1972, p. 365.

Fig. 9: Entry-Architecture: The Arch of Septimius Severus at the
Forum Romanum, constructed in 203 A.D. in memory of the vic-
tories over the Parthians.

defined as belief in the devil under secularised conditions. The
individual integrated in a premodern order still saw himself as
being in the centre of the processes around him. The future sig-
nified the reproduction of cosmic order. "Exposed to the devil's
temptation and subject to the grace of God, man could not gain
access to the unconscious. This appeared according to subjec-
tive appraisal to be either demonic or divine but always as an
external force."[60] It was not until the imaginary external center-
ing was abandoned through the Age of Enlightenment that an

[60] Mario Erdheim: "Einleitung: Freuds Erkundungen an den Grenzen zwischen Theorie und Wahn", in: Sigmund Freud: *Zwei Fallberichte*, Frankfurt am Main: Fischer,
1997, p. 16.

Fig. 10: Exit-Architecture: The triumphal arch was for the Romans what the panic column is for the present (montage by Stephan Trüby, Julian Friedauer).

inner paranoid space opened up in which all those energies resurfaced which had prior to this been isolated externally from the self. The greenhouse of paranoia was the interior of the Western world now without any dangers but riddled with risk.

The enemies within whether they be real or imaginary were always a risky matter. Fear of them has pervaded the modern age for much of the time, but with the denationalisation of warfare everywhere which the 20th century entailed it became the dominating phenomenon politically, culturally and of everyday self-assurance. Three quarters of all the wars in last 100 years have not been state wars but rather territorial or transnational wars.

Fig. 11: Belief in the devil under secularised conditions: Vincent Mazeau's "EVIL/EXIT Theater", 2003.

The epoch of nationalized wars can be considered to be over.[61] "The classic wars between states were usually decided in battles the outcome of which formed the basis of the ensuing peace agreement. In the new wars battles hardly take place and even peace agreements in their conventional form have become rare … if there is any chance at all to end a war then not by peace agreements but peace processes."[62]

---

[61] Cf. Münkler, *Über den Krieg*, p. 220.
[62] Herfried Münkler: "Die Neuen Kriege", in: *ARCH+*, No. 164/165, "Das Arsenal der Architektur", April 2003, p. 31.

The cross-fading of burning buildings and denationalised war is a result of the events of 11th September 2001. Before the twin towers of the World Trade Center (WTC) became ex-architecture they were certainly successful exit-architecture; the emergency routes saved thousands of peoples' lives. Ever since the collapse of the WTC high-rise architecture has changed perceptibly. "In the 80's it was questions concerning high-technology that came to the fore, then in the 90's it was sustainability, and with September 11th attention has now been drawn to security in skyscrapers. Security is dealt with on three levels. Clustering towers rather isolating them, dispersion of emergency routes rather than concentrating them and the use of sacrificial façades instead of curtain walls."[63] In addition to these new features it must be added that the designs submitted for the new building of Ground Zero were, for the first time in the history of architecture competitions, not only discussed from the standpoint of technology and aesthetic considerations but above from the standpoint of all the emergency routes – and this, to stress it, not by jurors but also by architecture critics.

At the moment when disciplinary society became control society and when security, internal or external, could no longer be guaranteed by the state, that is when exit routes were codified. The pre-modern rule adjustment of *decorum* still had a clear point of escape; it was the inner space where one could relax, the outer space was where the unconscious could project its divine or demonic personnel. The modern age with its enclosing environments had its clearly defined points of escape too. This was the pacified outer space accessible via the learning corridor where relaxation was possible and from then on it was the inner space where the unconscious could hatch out its paranoia. Ever since denationali-

---

[63] "Das Arsenal der Architektur. Friedrich Kittler und Alexander Kluge im Gespräch mit der ARCH+", in: *ARCH+*, No. 164/165, p. 27.

sation of wars has become the rule, i.e. since about the second half of the 20th century, the only movement which is safe is movement along escape routes which no longer have a point of escape.

The relentless vigilance of the paranoiac modern age has always applied to inner enemies whereas the somnolence of the 'Baldwinized' modern age has applied to external enemies. Both the somnolence and the vigilance flowed into the post-modern controlling society as a narcoleptic cocktail. Since that time periods of being asleep and being awake have been alternating rapidly. The latter are initiated by enculturating events guaranteeing an effective transfer: catastrophes.

2.4 Hertzianism: Design in the Third Machine Age

Architecture is a transgenerational copy-paste business under conditions of stress, the most extreme of which is the case of war. Pre-modern warring cultures copied the transmission units of *ornamentum* onto the next generation and modern disciplinary societies the transmission units of their claustrophobic specified ways.

Post-modern controlling societies in contrast copy their building codes onto the next generation. The exit-architectures of the present are codifications in an age of war which knows no difference between inner and outer anymore. Of course they do not begin with exit signs and do not end on the pavement next to the emergency exit.

Architectural codifications arise from phases of relaxation which are only effective in protective localities. If the pre-modern *decorum* rule adjustments provided a secure point of escape in the inner world and the modern institutional typologies understood the outer world as a kind of 'wellness zone', then the question must be asked as to the points of relaxation in times of omnipresently perceived stressors. Where and how is one supposed to relax on escape routes?

If the new wars can be said to be pervasive, then one can expect that pervasive stressors generate pervasive protective space. The idea of pervasive protective space shakes the supposed foundations of architecture, those that differentiate between internal and external. The gadget could become the crystallizing point of such a pervasive protective space. The term 'gadget' is derived from the French *gâchette* (the catch of a lock or bolt). With all probability the gadget linked to the pervasive game of terror and the war on terror is becoming a key element of a pervasive architecture. The gadget is a key element because it unlocks data and information. It ensures access by means of fetishism.

Fetishes are objects which have at their disposal what is called 'agency', a word alternating between freedom of will and radiation intensity. The Pidgin word *fetisso* is closely associated with Portuguese colonial history in Africa which had its beginnings in the 15th century.[64] In the traditional systems of religion and customs the European conquerors encountered numerous objects which they supposed to be the agency of the devil. But the idea that certain objects could have such power was only a distorted European picture of the Christian cult of saints and relics which had been in full sway since the late Middle Ages but was being vehemently combated by the church. That which the Portuguese discredited on the distant shores of Africa was that which was forbidden in their own culture.

---

[64] Cf. Karl-Heinz Kohl: *Die Macht der Dinge: Geschichte und Theorie sakraler Objekte*, Munich: C. H. Beck, 2003, and Hartmut Böhme: *Fetischismus und Kultur. Eine andere Theorie der Moderne*, Reinbek bei Hamburg: Rowohlt, 2006.

Four hundred years later the fetish ended up in the centre of European culture and again in a forbidden zone, this time as commodity fetishism. It was Karl Marx especially who tried to stop it. A commodity, he wrote in 1867, is "a very queer thing, abounding in metaphysical subtleties and theological niceties."[65] Marx justifies the fetishist character of the commodity that it gives the impression of being in itself enhancing. The fact that manpower is behind the making of the commodity has according to Marx been wrongly forgotten: "Just as the user of the fetish personifies the object of his cult and expects supernatural results from it, so does the capitalistic society regard capital as a self-actualising force which creates new values and wondrously multiplies"[66] The self-actualisation of the exchange value as opposed to the use value had become some mysterious agency.

Design became the agent for this agency. Designers were needed as in the wake of industrialization the individual craftsmen lost control of it.[67] Experts in fetishism were required, experts who were able to comprehend the manufacturing process from its conception right up to its marketing. This change had already taken place in many industries in the 18th century but it was not until 1907 with the founding of the Deutscher Werkbund in Munich that design made a determined effort to hook up with industry, this was so to say the moment of birth for industrial design.[68]

Since this time industry has been concerned with one dramatically unanswered question: What exactly makes one product more successful than another one? One of the most robust pref-

---

[65] Karl Marx: *Das Kapital*, Vol. 1, Marx-Engels-Werke No. 23, Berlin/DDR: Dietz, 1956., p. 85.

[66] Kohl, *Die Macht der Dinge*, p. 96.

[67] Cf. Adrian Forty: *Objects of Desire: Design and Society since 1750*, London: Thames & Hudson, 1986, p. 29.

[68] Cf. Norbert Bolz: *Bang-Design. Design-Manifest des 21. Jahrhunderts*, Hamburg: Trendbüro, 2006, p. 31.

erence theories originates from the cultural anthropologists Robert Boyd and Peter J. Richerson. They differentiate between indicator traits and preference traits.[69] By indicator traits they mean artefacts or rules which safeguard survival at definite moments of crisis, and by preference traits they mean artefacts or rules which remind one of indicator traits. These belong to the relaxation phase, for example shopping; those to the stress phase, for example war. According to Boyd and Richerson as soon as people start to relax they want to buy the indicator trait, which stands for war, as a preference trait.

The nexus of survival and buying preference runs like a leitmotif through the entire history of design and consumption. Two examples: Charles and Ray Eames developed in the Second World War a leg splint of plywood which enabled the transport of some 150,000 wounded soldiers; thereupon the success could begin for the Eames Chair, which not only relied on the constructional techniques using plywood but also due to its similarities with the indicator characteristics of the leg splint [Figs. 12, 13]. And then there was Paul Virilio who in the 60's analysed the Nazi-bunkers of the German Atlantic wall and together with Claude Parent built a church in Nevers exactly in the form of the detested Organisation Todt, which was responsible for the Atlantic wall's construction. One may regard these examples as effusive exceptions to the rule or not, but the fact is that many marketable design products often have a very close resemblance to military artefacts. The fashion world especially is full of militarily based preferential characteristics. For example the camouflage pattern, which every youth culture apparently has not been able to do without since the 90's, marks the preliminary culmination of a long liaison be-

---

[69]   Cf. Richard Boyd and Peter J. Richerson: *Culture and the Evolutionary Process*, University of Chicago Press, Chicago, 1985.

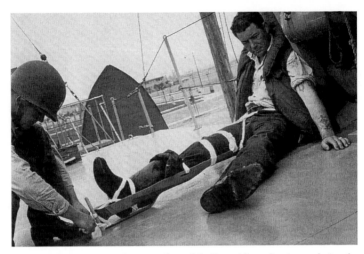

Fig. 12: Indicator traits make survival possible: Eames' leg splint in use during the Second World War.

tween consumer behaviour and bellicose innuendo. It is in this context immaterial to whether the punks' Gestapo coats and the hippie's parkas were intended subversively, but what is of primary significance are the explicit preferences for *that* particular coat, *that* particular design for a church or specific chair irrespective of implicit motives.

If it is true that we prefer to buy symbols of survival when shopping, i.e. if there is an *ornamentum* of fitness for war, then the question must be raised; is there a *decorum* of the present? And if so: How is it transmitted?

"War is the father of all things" is Heracleitus's controversial adage; written 2,500 years ago it seems to have lost none of its relevance. In fact it is almost impossible to find but one innovative product whose development or manufacture does not have its origins in war. From the steam locomotive whose

Fig. 13: Preference traits remind us of indicator traits: Charles Eames relaxing in the Eames chair.

creation is inseparable from cannon construction, to the computer tomograph whose existence is inconceivable without the US military's microprocessors and on to GPS which would not be there if there were no Pentagon. Everywhere war marks the beginning of export trade at the end of which a high-tech product awaits which will be available generally. And when Vilém Flusser wrote, "that everything (or nearly everything) is a technical acquisition resulting from war, that we are in this sense all war-damaged, and that if we made love and not war everything would vanish and we would surface or submerge in the peace of an immaterial world"[70] – when he wrote this even the immaterial world itself was no longer a peaceful one.

This is because at the end of the 19th century the imaginary agency of successful design – survival or fitness in war – was

---

[70] Vilém Flusser : "Vom Vater aller Dinge" (http://www.khm.de/flusser/material.html; 19 July 2007).

increasingly supported and justified by research in physics. The discovery of the existence of the electromagnetic spectrum by Heinrich Hertz in Karlsruhe in 1888 contributed much to this. He was able to prove with his 'Hertz oscillator' that electromagnetic waves are discharged at the same speed as light. As a result fundamental certainties as to the way we perceive the world and the laws of physics became less sure. Not only did this pave the way for future radio engineering but also our understanding of things for which this formed a basis of reference in dynamic processes and energy fields.[71] Thus, visible light, at one time divine, was degraded to a small segment of a much larger array of wavelengths. Thanks to Hertz do we now know that the electromagnetic spectrum spans from low energy radio waves to high energy gamma rays and between these extremes there are microwaves, infrared, ultraviolet, X-rays etc.

"The winner of the next war will be the one who best understands how to utilize the electromagnetic spectrum",[72] Admiral Sergei G. Gorshkov prophesied after the Second World War – and he was right. Ever since the 20th century, in addition to the earth's surface be it land or water, we now have three new strategic spaces; underwater space, aerospace and cyberspace. It is the last one which exhibits a great degree of co-extensity with the electromagnetic spectrum.

The cybersphere is that strategic space which will prove decisive in waging the new wars because it allows partisan and guerrilla strategies in military strategic thought. The Israeli military operations in the Jenin refugee camp in 2002 will serve as an example. The soldiers of the Israeli Defence Forces (IDF),

---

[71]   Böhme, *Fetischismus und Kultur*, p. 141.
[72]   Quoted after Thomas Miessgang: "Pixelparade in der Feuerwüste", in: *Attack! Kunst und Krieg in den Zeiten der Medien*, exhibition catalogue, ed. by Kunsthalle Wien, Göttingen: Steidl, 2003, p. 13.

armed to the teeth with tracking systems and high-tech gadgets etc., did not, for reasons of security, move through the streets and alleys but rather bombed and gouged their way in loose swarm formation through the walls and roofs of Arab houses.[73] MOUT soldiers ('MOUT' stands for Military Operations in Urbanized Terrains) can be considered 'close relatives' of the IDF soldiers. They represent the platform of an electromagnetic field, the core elements of their equipment are to be found in their backpacks e.g. computer unit, transmitter, battery, GPS; in their helmets cameras and displays.[74] Orientation by means of a monocular display enables the soldier to read maps, give and take orders, make progress reports and to stay in touch with his superior and his group by e-mail at all times. Sensors and motion detectors are used to mark enemy targets, mobiles and monitors serve as the basis for internal communication and multilingual translation computers facilitate understanding with the local population.[75]

Ever since the electromagnetic spectrum has started trying to confirm the agency of fetishism, many commodities have been leading double lives; half artefact, half data. Slowly but surely the vision of the 'network of things', from which Mark Weiser spoke in 1991 in reference to an age of ubiquitous computing, is becoming reality.[76] When Reyner Banham in 1960 analysed the design of the First Machine Age he had larger more he-

---

[73] Cf. "Krieg der Städte – Eyal Weizman im Gespräch mit Philipp Misselwitz", in: *ARCH+*, No. 164/165, April 2003, pp. 68-69.

[74] Cf. Drehli Robnik and Siegfried Mattl: "'No one else is gonna die!' Urban warriors und andere Ausnahmefälle in neuen Kriegen und Blockbustern", in: *Attack! Kunst und Krieg in den Zeiten der Medien*, exhibition catalogue, ed. by Kunsthalle Wien, Göttingen: Steidl, 2003, p. 45.

[75] Ibid.

[76] Mark Weiser: "The Computer for the 21st Century" (http://www.ubiq.com/hypertext/weiser/SciAmDraft3.html; 19 July 2007).

roic hardware such as planes and automobiles in mind.[77] Thirty years later, as Martin Pawley spoke of the design of the Second Machine Age, the machines had already undergone a downsizing e.g. washing machines and vacuum cleaners.[78] By 2005, as Anthony Dunne spoke of the Third Machine Age, the focus was on things whose potential was not immediately obvious at first sight: "Objects not only 'dematerialise' into software in response to miniaturization and replacement by services, but literally dematerialise into radiation. All electronic products are hybrids of radiation and matter."[79]

In architecture too, a movement towards what could be termed 'Hertzianism' has become increasingly apparent. A growing sensitivity to things electromagnetic has become not only evident in facility management, i.e. in the communication between increasingly more intelligent architecture and professional building management, but also in the interaction between the building and its user. Thus in 2006 the Parisian architect François Roche suggested linking gadget to building for a new museum of architecture in Orléans, in which visitors would find their way through a labyrinth-like house which would continually be rerouted by a robot by means of a PDA. Such tendencies are reinforced by developments in research in ambient intelligence. Although such marketable applications are still in short supply at present, there have certainly been developments in transport and textile technologies which will, sooner or later, find their way into architecture. So it is only a question of time until intelligent carpets or wall hangings equipped with motion

[77] Reyner Banham: *Theory and Design in the First Machine Age*, London: The Architectural Press, 1960.

[78] Martin Pawley: *Theory and Design in the Second Machine Age*, Oxford/Cambridge, Mass.: Blackwell, 1990.

[79] Anthony Dunne: *Hertzian Tales: Electronic Products, Aesthetic Experience, and Critical Design*, Cambridge, Mass./London: The MIT Press, 2005, p. 101

detectors or fire detectors woven into them become signposts with LEDs.

The pervasive architecture of the Third Machine Age is Hertzian. It consists of large and small gadgets (building parts and PDAs), all held coherently together by the electromagnetic spectrum. Complementing the escape chreodes of the building codes, the Hertzian gadgets form an exit architecture which only recognizes ephemeral pseudotribal swarming structures and attempts to escape which lie beyond the categories of internal and external. And as everyone knows from James Bond films, he who is always on the run appreciates handy technical support: "Gadgets are assigned to the mobile hero whether infiltrating or fleeing."[80]

But in contrast to James Bond those who are mobilized at the present time are everything but heroes. The new pervasive wars do not end anymore. During the Second Iraq War in 2003, 171 coalition soldiers died whereas 'after' the war the figure was 3,900, not to mention members of the Iraqi armed forces and civilians. What the new wars have in common with the pre-modern epoch of *decorum* is that they are sensed culturally even in the area outside the field of combat and moreover they offer no relaxation. Nothing could be more unfitting at the present time as triumphal processions and confetti parades on Times Square. In the place of the *ornamentum* aglow with good fortune of antiquity, the consumer product with its bellicose preference traits emerges. The store shelves from Sak's in Fifth Avenue to Safeway are the *decorum* of our times.

---

[80] Georg Seeßlen: "War Rooms, Casinos & Gadgets: Die mythische Konstruktion der Bauten von Ken Adam", in: Jürgen Berger (ed.): *Ken Adam. Production Design, Meisterwerke der Filmarchitektur*, Munich/Mannheim: SFK-Verband and Landesmuseum für Technik und Arbeit, 1994, p. 21.

How is this *decorum* transmitted transgenerationally? By means of paranoiac vigilance. Just as the exit chreodes pave their way through the transgenerational terrain of the Baldwinized somnolence by means of risk evaluation, so does the range of products. And the Hertzian artefacts allow themselves to be transmitted the best. This is because paranoia is always also negative assessment of technological consequences as can be seen in James Tilly Matthews' "Air Loom" or in Daniel Paul Schreber's "Rays of God". Schreber, on whose case study Freud based his famous theories on paranoia, was certified between 1895 and 1898. In this time Röntgen discovered X-rays in 1895, and Becquerel discovered radioactivity in 1896. For Schreber rays disintegrate the subject's autonomy and make him the object of manipulation.[81] Not only here does paranoia prove to be a gigantic technological fantasy pointing to the electronic simulations of the 20th century.[82] Our senses have become 'agents of misrepresentation' and it is up to a Hertzian architecture to create a vital advantage from the anaesthetic.[83]

3. War-/Peace-Architectures

Cultural evolutionary theory depopulates the heavens of exceptional performance. It not only puts the meaning of individual architects into perspective but also individual pieces of architecture. The question is however, is there something like a solitary highly concentrated edifice – individual pieces of architecture which are able to transmit differential traits more strongly?

---

[81] Christoph Asendorf: *Ströme und Strahlen. Das langsame Verschwinden der Materie um 1900*, Gießen: Anabas, 1989, p. 140.

[82] Cf. Asendorf, *Ströme und Strahlen*, p. 141.

[83] On the relationship between aesthetics and anaesthetics see Wolfgang Welsch: *Ästhetisches Denken*, Stuttgart: Reclam, 1990, p. 19.

Three examples of architecture will now be examined none of which is in the normal sense of historical representation 'significant architecture'. Only one of the buildings has arisen in a secular context, the other two are associated with religious traditions. In all three, ways, routes or paths play an important role.

The first example is the Roman Temple of Janus, a key building of antiquity. Even in the period of the Eighty Years' War and the Thirty Years' War, i.e. in the 18th century its influence was to be keenly felt. Thus this building marked the transmission to the epoch of legally defined wars which modern nationalism entailed. The end of this era is landmarked by the second example: the Pentagon in Arlington near Washington D.C. The third and last example, the Jamarat Bridge in Mina near Mecca, seems at first glance to be the odd man out as in this case it is a purely infrastructural building whose function is to facilitate the performance of a religious ritual. However, the Jamarat Bridge, as this thesis seeks to demonstrate, is deeply enrooted in the violence of *all* monotheistic religions and plays a role which should not be underestimated in the Islamic theory of the Holy War.

3.1 Temple of Janus (Forum Romanum)

If there has ever been a direct link between architecture and war then it must surely be the Temple of Janus. Its doors stood open when the Imperium Romanum was waging war and they were shut when peace prevailed.

Janus must be considered the mythical primordial king of Latium and thus stands at the beginnings of the history of Rome.[84]

---

[84] Cf. Thomas Ganschow: *Krieg in der Antike*, Darmstadt: Primus, 2007, p. 150.

There he is said not only to have introduced civilization but also to have founded the temples to the gods. That is why Janus, the 'god of the gods', was the first to be called upon in all religious ceremonies and rituals.

Janus also stood at the beginning of various official and private matters. As the god of initiation he was present at every birth, and all temporal transitions from the new year to the beginning of the month and dawn and dusk were dedicated to him. In the 7th century BC the month January was named after him. Initially this month was the eleventh in the year but through the reform of the calendar by Tarquinius Priscus it became the first.

Eventually the god of temporal matters became the god of spatial passages: Janus the god of gates, bridges, paths and the doors of houses (*ianuae*). And just as doors do, Janus proves to have two sides. He was first depicted on coins Servius Tullius had minted in the 5th century BC, showing a double face god looking forwards and backwards (thus the epithets Geminus, Bifrons, Biceps).[85] Janus even appears with four heads on Hadrian's coins from the 2nd century BC.

Many buildings were dedicated to Janus, but only one was to have such momentous consequence for the entire population of the Roman empire: the Temple of Janus Geminus also known as Janus Quirinus. No findings of this building have ever been announced but the building probably stood at the north eastern end of the Forum Romanum in a street called Argiletum which ran between the Basilica Aemilia and the Curia. It was probably one of the oldest buildings on the spot.

---

[85] This tradition was interpreted as being inherited from images of Hermes which commonly displayed a double head. – Cf. Bessie Rebecca Burchett: *Janus in Roman Life and Cult. Studies in Roman Religion*, Menasha, Wisconsin: George Banta, 1918, p. 28.

Fig. 14: War-/Peace-Architecture:
The Temple of Janus of antiquity
on a coin from Nero's reign.

The Temple of Janus was by no means a magnificent building but hardly more than a decorated passageway with two sets
of double doors pointing in an easterly direction and a west-
erly direction respectively. According to various traditions the
building was erected in the 7th century BC by Numa Pompilius
the legendary second king of Rome.[86] The introduction of the
custom of opening the doors of the temple at times of war is also
attributed to him. Thanks to coins from the time of Augustus
and Nero and a description by Procopius from the 6th century
AD we have a good idea of what its architecture must have been
like. According to Procopius the temple consisted of ore, was
cuboid and just high enough to accommodate a bronze statue of
Janus [Fig. 14]. The two sets of ornately adorned double doors
were fitted between four Corinthian columns on which rested
the arched or horizontal lintels. The masonry side walls were
covered by a latticework draped with wreaths of plants. The
faces of Janus peered in the direction of the two doorways.

In the thousand years of history of the Imperium Romanum the
Temple of Janus was rarely locked. Its doors apparently stood
open after the time of Numa for half a century and didn't close

---

[86] Cf. Burchett, *Janus in Roman Life and Cult*, p. 39.

again until after the First Punic War of 235 BC.[87] Under Augustus and his Pax Romana the building was closed more often, he had the temple locked up at least three times if not four.[88] The first time he did this was after the Battle of Actium on the 12th January 29 BC (changing his name from Octavian to Augustus on the following day). The next time he closed the temple was in 25 BC when victory over the Cantabri brought the Spanish Wars to an end, and the third time was 9 BC after triumphing against the Parthians.[89] It was not until Nero that doors were closed again, and then possibly under Domitian, with certainty under Marcus Aurelius and Commodus and then under Consantine and Honorius. The last authenticated closure of the Temple of Janus occurred in the 5th century AD, and the building vanished together with the Roman Empire.[90]

The Temple of Janus represents a remarkable cultural instrument simultaneously manipulating the population to preparedness for war and a longing for peace. The Roman's mobilisation occurred by means of a declaration of war which was enforced with sacral legitimacy. In front of the temple was a piece of land which was declared to be enemy territory by a fetial (priest) throwing a spear. And then the 'Portals of War' were opened under the gaze of Janus and the furore spread throughout the

---

[87] "13. Janus Quirinus, which our ancestors ordered to be closed whenever there was peace, secured by victory, throughout the whole domain of the Roman people on land and sea, and which, before my birth is recorded to have been closed but twice in all since the foundation of the city, the senate ordered to be closed thrice while I was princeps" – Quoted after: *The Achievements of the Divine Augustus (Res gestae divi Augusti)*.

[88] Cf. Burchett, *Janus in Roman Life and Cult*, p. 39.

[89] This historic moment is the background to Reinhard Keiser's Opera *Der bey dem allgemeinen Welt-Friede von dem Grossen Augustus geschlossene Tempel des JANUS* (1698). – Cf. Dorothea Schröder: *Zeitgeschichte auf der Opernbühne. Barockes Musiktheater in Hamburg im Dienst von Politik und Diplomatie (1690-1745)*, Göttingen: Vandenhoeck & Ruprecht, 1998, p. 94.

[90] Cf. Burchett, *Janus in Roman Life and Cult*, p. 40.

entire country. It was important that the spatial passageway of the opened temple could always be regarded in terms of a temporal phase. "The escalation of fury activated all collective and individual reserves in fitness", says Ulrich Heinen about the Janus cult.[91] "Only in an occasional state of emergency can a culture dare to do this because it jeopardizes all its consistent characteristics in such phases and risks not being able to simulate the sense of security essential for the vital relaxation phase from which its coherence and its ability to give birth to traditions depend after such an escalation."[92]

It has been said that temples are architectures of stress and triumphal arches are architectures of relaxation. The Temple of Janus was both stress and relaxation architecture and thus is able to shed some light on the previous history of Roman triumphal arches. This is because it represents the first example in Roman history of a purely symbolic piece of architecture preconceived as a channel. This channel represented the borderline between that which was Rome and that which was not Rome.

In the beginnings of the Roman period of kings the Temple of Janus formed a city gate to a settlement preceding Rome, the legend of the rape of the Sabine women indicates this. As the Sabines tried to storm Rome it was easy at first as the city gates opened of their own accord (according to Ovid opened the gate as this goddess was ill disposed towards the Romans). As the defenders could no longer hold the open gate Janus is supposed to have hurled a great mass of boiling water at the attackers through the open gate. Rome was saved and so the curious custom of leaving the doors of the temple open at times of war is

---

[91]   Ulrich Heinen: "Friedenssehnsucht als Antrieb der europäischen Weltfriedenskulptur: Vergils Aeneis und Europa", in: Bazon Brock and Gerlinde Koschik (eds.): *Krieg + Kunst*, Munich: Wilhelm Fink, 2002, p. 170.
[92]   Ibid.

Fig. 15: Rubens' Temple of Janus, designed for Ferdinand of Habsburg's entry into Antwerp (1635).

said to have arisen. As of that day the army always passed in and out of this gate in times of war. With Rome's increasing success in war the construction migrated from the periphery to the centre of territory conquered. From the combination of proto-triumphal arch and gate as a starting point, from the place were armies sallied forth and returned home remained some hundred years later only an area for symbolic declarations of war, gates catering to specific wars had long ago taken over the tasks of the cultural relaxation phase.

The Temple of Janus stood for an idea of peace which would have been inconceivable without Roman dominance. This changed dramatically as the Janus motif, which survived the decline of Rome well, was transferred to modern times. Here it came up against a new phenomenon, namely the concept of cross-national peace.

It was above all Rubens who understood how to revitalize the Janus motif in the 17th century. This may be due to the fact that no other artist of the age was so active in promoting peace.[93] For over a decade from 1623 until 1635 Rubens was diplomatically active, initially under the cloak of his artistic activities for secret peace negotiations within the Netherlands and later as an official envoy when he concluded a peace treaty in London in 1630. His sphere of influence was the the final phase of the Eighty Years War which like the Thirty Years War was ended by the Westphalian Peace Treaties of 1648.

Rubens first made reference to the Temple of Janus motif in 1627 as a book illustration.[94] Eight years later he made use of it again in the decorations which he designed in 1635 for Cardinal-Infante Ferdinand von Habsburg's entry in Antwerp who was to be the new Spanish governor of the Netherlands [Fig. 15]. "If former entries had shown governors where war was

---

[93]   Cf. Hans-Martin Kaulbach: "Peter Paul Rubens: Diplomat und Maler des Friedens", in: *1648: Krieg und Frieden in Europa*, Münster, Vol. 2: Kunst und Kultur, exhibition catalogue, Münster: 1998.

[94]   In this year it became clear that peace between the Netherlands and Spain could not be achieved by any direct means. Rubens had already represented this constellation of tensions in 1623 on two title pages for a book on the history of the Netherlands. For the third volume, the history of the uprising of 1560 until the twelve-year ceasefire Rubens dramatized the scene: The text is on a curtain which conceals the interior of the Temple of Janus. "Discordia, Fury and other personifications of the horrors of war wrench the doors open – the worst, the outbreak of war destroying everything in its wake is imminent." – Cf. Kaulbach, "Peter Paul Rubens: Diplomat und Maler des Friedens".

73

surmounted, Ferdinand found himself directly confronted with the outbreak and horror of war: The fury of war stormed through the opened doors of the Temple of Janus, while Pax, Pietas and the archduchess Isabella compel the observer to close the doors again."[95] The difference to the Roman triumph could not have been greater, the times of pure relaxation were over. Even during the triumphal entry came the admonishment of the perils of war and eye-witnesses were even implored to close the doors of the Temple of Janus.

3.2 Pentagon (Arlington, Virginia)

It was the development of the atom bomb which enabled the breakthrough for a post-modern epoch of denationalised wars. This is because if wars do not need to be waged anymore but only have to be conceived then the possibility to safeguard one's own population dwindles. The consequence of which is, where the state no longer can guarantee the safety of its citizens their willingness to obey and follow is eroded.[96]

The change in paradigms from nationalized to denationalised warfare left a gigantic building in its wake – the Pentagon in Arlington near Washington D.C. [Fig. 16]. It was built with the purpose of winning nothing less than the Second World War. Its completion marks the emergence of the first atomic super power. The Pentagon is not only the largest building in the world but also its design and construction are unsurpassed in the speed in which they were carried out. It was Brigadier General Brehon B. Somervell, head of the construction department of the US Army, who took the initiative for its construction in the year

---

[95] Ibid.
[96] Cf. Münkler, *Über den Krieg*, p. 210.

Fig. 16: Hypostasis of centrality: The Pentagon in Arlington near Washington D.C. (constructed 1941-1943).

1941. The War Ministry urgently needed a new building as at that time 24,000 ministry employees were dispersed in seventeen different buildings. What had been a mere inconvenience in times of peace had now become a threat in a time of national crisis. On Thursday evening of the 17th July Somervell ordered that the plans for an efficient, working war ministry should be on his desk by 9 o'clock on the following Monday morning.[97] The deadline was met. Within one week Somervell and his staff not only managed to produce the drafts for the largest building in the world, not only managed to gain the support of the entire war ministry, including a very sceptical war minister, but also got the go-ahead from the US President himself.[98]

[97] Cf. Steve Vogel: *The Pentagon. A History*, New York: Random House, 2007, p. xxiv.
[98] Ibid., p. 45.

George Edwin Bergström was appointed chief architect for the Pentagon.[99] The pentagonal design is said to have been his idea and apparently he had no problems in getting this idea accepted as Somervell liked the fact that the form reminded him of traditional fortress architecture like Fort Sunter from the time of the Civil War.[100] Roosevelt too, announced his liking for Bergström's proposals. "You know, gentlemen", he said on 2nd September in 1941, "I like that pentagon-shaped building. You know why? I like it because nothing like this has ever been done that way before."[101]

On 11th September 1941, not even two months after Somervell had announced his intentions, construction work began.[102] There was no ceremony, no photographs, absolutely nothing. Everybody simply got down to work. Bergstöm's workforce consisted of 110 architects, 54 structural engineers, 43 mechanical engineers, 18 electrical engineers, 13 drainage experts and a number of other specialists.[103] There was total chaos on the gigantic site because the planners working in a disused aeroplane hanger were behind schedule with their drawings. The extent of organisational problems was immense and the pressure on the individual too. Two architects died of heart attacks,[104] two construction workers in accidents involving concrete, one worker is supposed to have been discovered cast in cement,[105] the other is said to have fallen in a ditch full of concrete which not set yet. The idea of fishing him out of the gooey mass was immediately abandoned as rescuers would have arrived too late anyway.

[99] Ibid., p. 38.
[100] Ibid., p. 114.
[101] Ibid., p. 117.
[102] Ibid., p. 126.
[103] Ibid., p. 149.
[104] Ibid., p. 176.
[105] Ibid., p. 197.

At the end of this chaotic period an extraordinary layout of corridors had been produced. In spite of the fact that the total length of corridors amounted to 17.5 miles (28.2 kilometres) one only needed a maximum of seven minutes to reach one point from another. Admittedly this kind of architecture initially had its drawbacks as far as orientation was concerned. The magazine *Life* compared Pentagon staff with rats in a behavioural scientist's labyrinth.[106] Eisenhower himself lost his way trying to get back to his office: "I walked and walked, encountering neither landmarks nor people who looked familiar. One had to give the building his grudging admiration; it had apparently been designed to confuse any enemy who might infiltrate it."[107] Finally a shorthand typist conveyed the President back to his desk. Only the *Architectural Forum* was more convinced and wrote in 1943: "Here is the picture of a future architecture in which building will be linked to their users by smooth-flowing traffic networks."[108]

Somervell also had a deputy, Leslie R. Groves by name, who had been entrusted with the organization of the construction site and who proved to be an extremely efficient and stalwart manager. After just a few months at the site he was promoted to military director of the Manhattan Project – that formidable and top-secret research project which eventually was to produce the atom bomb and thus bring about the end of the 2nd World War. While still working at the Pentagon site Groves is supposedly to have said about the stress there: "I was hoping to get to a war theatre so I could find a little peace."[109]

War as peace, peace as war – Groves' paradox anticipated the political and military developments of the coming decades

---

[106] Ibid., p. 290.
[107] Ibid., pp. 329-30.
[108] Ibid., p. 302.
[109] Leslie R. Groves, quoted after Vogel, *The Pentagon*, p. 258.

which provoked extreme opposites to coincide with one another. The Cold War was in fact a war which, due to the fact that it only took place in everybody's minds, took place everywhere. Even in the remotest areas the atomic bomb posed a deadly threat. Thus the Pentagon marks the final hypostasis of centrality before decentralizing tendencies in military thinking took the floor. The development of ARPAnet, the precursor to the Internet which cleverly linked scattered headquarters with leading US universities, would have been inconceivable without the nuclear threat.[110]

The substitution of the one large centre through many small centres starts with the most important war room in the Pentagon. During the First World War the US War Departments were to a large extent stationed in France, in the Second World War however, the majority of Allied military operations were increasingly supervised from Washington.[111] Worldwide operations pivoted around the so-called Signal Center on the fifth floor of the inner Pentagon ring. The largest communications facility of its time, this elegant room with its fluorescent surfaces, was able to transmit five million words per day.[112] The Signal Center was the ultimate 'centre in the periphery'.

And the last of its kind. For the atom bomb had made a farce of centrality. In the Pentagon's central courtyard used to be a legendary kiosk during the Cold War whose coordinates were in the sights of Russian nuclear warheads at all times. The Soviets mistakenly assumed that the technological nerve centre of the entire complex was concealed under this small building. In fact it was just a hot-dog stand called Café Ground Zero by

---

[110] Friedrich Kittler: "Von Städtern und Nomaden", in: Brock and Koschik, *Krieg + Kunst*, p. 11.
[111] Cf. Vogel, *The Pentagon*, p. 184.
[112] Ibid., p. 273.

Fig. 17: Centrality as a farce: The hot dog stand in the central courtyard of the Pentagon, pulled down in 2006.

the Pentagon staff [Fig. 17]. It was torn down in 2006 but a new building with similar proportions will be opened soon.

3.3 Jamarat Bridge (Mina near Mecca)

"God is dead! God remains dead! And we have killed him! How shall we comfort ourselves?" wrote Friedrich Nietzsche in 1882.[113] God declared dead however is alive and kicking because many of our brains do not wish it so.

Religion is a transgenerational imitative behaviour the analysis of which by theoretical evolutionary means seems obvious.[114]

---

[113] Friedrich Nietzsche: *The Gay Science*, 1882.
[114] Cf. Heiner Mühlmann: *Jesus überlistet Darwin*, Vienna/New York: Springer, 2007

Transmission theory has paid considerable attention to the ritual which it sees as a stress induced enculturating unit. "Rituals which activate the episodic memory to a large degree e.g. by stimulating the emotional episodic memory have the best chance of suffering no mnemotechnical damage when being transmitted."[115]

Of all religions Islam is at present the 'fittest'. A strong vertical transmission (large numbers of children) is evident in that part of the world strongly influenced by Islam and for non-Muslim countries a strong horizontal transmission (conversion).

In many Islamic orientated countries dominant religiousness certainly impedes the critical variants of scientific introspection. Thus an analysis of pilgrims going to Mecca from perspectives of cultural and religious evolution has not yet been possible. "Muslims", writes Mohammed Arkoun, "have up to now only taken vertical dimensions into consideration in regards to the Hajj as prescribed by the Quran which in the dogma of the 'messenger sent down by God' (*tanzil*) revelation is to be found on earth."[116] In contrast the horizontal dimension of the sociological and historical circumstances, which have enabled the transition from heathen to the Islamic Hajj, have been eclipsed: "For the growing flocks of pilgrims coming to Mecca every year any historical or anthropological enquiry into the Hajj is unthinkable if not outrageous."[117]

It is above all, one specific building which may throw some light onto recent transmission of Islamic religiousness. The building in question is the Jamarat Bridge in Mina near Mecca

---

[115] Mühlmann, *Jesus überlistet Darwin*, p. 37.
[116] Mohamed Arkoun: "Der Haddsch im islamischen Denken", in: Mohamed Ben Smail (ed.): *Pilgerfahrt nach Mekka*, Zurich/Freiburg im Breisgau: Atlantis, 1978, p. 13.
[117] Ibid.

Fig. 18: The world's most dangerous work of architecture: The first Jamarat Bridge, constructed 1975, demolished in 2006.

which has played an important role in the Hajj since the mid 70's. There used to be an Jamarat Bridge and soon there will be a new one. Whether the new bridge, which has been under construction since 2006, will likewise leave its mark on Islam as its predecessor is left to be seen.

The first Jamarat Bridge, which was in reality a viaduct, was erected in 1975 and demolished in 2006 [Fig. 18] as it was in its dilapidated state a risk to life and limb. Of all architectures it was without doubt the most perilous: More than one thousand pilgrims met their ends. They died by attempting to throw a certain number of pebbles at the three pillars representing the devil (*Jamara*) as prescribed in the Hajj ritual.

For hundreds of years these pillars had been at the side of a path going through the desert in the valley of Mina. At some time a village became established around them [Fig. 19]. By the 20th century the stream of pilgrims passing them had become

Fig. 19: The village of Mina with one of the devil's pillars, around 1950.

so immense that the houses were becoming more and more of a nuisance. In the 70's attempts were made to channel the crowds firstly with corrugated iron safety fences running through the village.[118] With the result that the pilgrims injured themselves on them. A solution had to be found!

And so it came to pass that a kind of motorway flyover was built for millions of pedestrians. Thereby death aura met banal straight-in-the-face architecture. Nowhere else in the world has the sublime teamed up with trash in such a holy alliance as was in the case of the Jamarat Bridge. Whoever claimed responsibility for this architecture remains unknown.

Mass deaths began in 1994 when 266 people died north of the Jamarah Al-Soughra [Fig. 20]. Three years later in 1997 22 people died on the northern side of the east entrance, the following year it was 118 pilgrims at the same place. In 2001 35 believers met their ends just north of the Jamarah Al-Kubra (also known as the „Great Jamara") and in 2004 249 people

---

[118] Cf. Bodo Rasch: *Zeltstädte*, IL 29, Stuttgart: Karl Krämer, 1980, pp. 100-101.

Fig. 20: Up to ten people per square metre: Crowds of pilgrims on the first Jamarat Bridge, 1979.

again at the same place. All were either crushed or trampled to death. "God is always able to make things easier for us", Abdellah Hammoudi once remarked, "why don't they make stoning easier?"[119]

After the deaths in 2004 the Saudi government decided to rebuild the bridge and to install an anti-panic tuning until the bridge's proposed demolition in 2006. Based on recommendations by Keith Still (Crowd Dynamics Ltd.) the devil's pillars mutated to devil's walls; the exit was widened from 20 to 40 meters on the west side, additional evacuation wings were created on the northern and southern sides and new emergency staircases on the eastern side [Fig. 21]. Furthermore an electronic control system was installed which was supposed to warn

---

[119] Abdellah Hammoudi: *Saison in Mekka. Geschichte einer Pilgerfahrt* (2005), Munich: Beck, 2007, p. 246.

Fig. 21: Safety tuning: The first Jamarat Bridge after renovation in 2004.

pilgrims of overcrowding. But all in vain, during the Hajj of 2006 two million people took part and again 363 people died.

Due to the large number of catastrophes the Jamarat Bridge became a favourite test track for international panic research. How could crowds of people be effectively controlled without creating new dangers? Why does it come to mass panic in the first place? Such questions among many others attracted the attention of Dirk Helbing, Anders Johansson and Habib Zein Al-Abideen, to mention but a few.[120] They discovered by means of video analyses and simulation models that in the case of dense crowds in contrast to traffic things did not come to a stand-still as in a traffic jam but instead completely the opposite. It is the unimaginable concentration of the crowds which have

---

[120] Dirk Helbing, Anders Johansson und Habib Zein Al-Abideen (2007): "The Dynamics of Crowd Disasters: An Empirical Study", in: *Physical Review* E 75, 046109 (arxiv.org/pdf/physics/0701203).

been measured for example on the Jamarat Bridge, 10 people per square meter, in which emergent self-movements ('crowd panic') sets in leading to casualties. Anti-panic architecture, according to the results of their research, consists of building blocks which reduce the pressure caused by the crowds without impeding movement to any extent – obstacles, zigzagging or undulated 'wavebreaks', forests of columns etc. That which at first glance seems to be something that would inhibit any means of escape can, if correctly positioned, work wonders.

The area around the Jamarat Bridge is according to Islamic tradition the place where Abraham, his slave Hagar and their son Ismail endorsed, against the greatest resistance, monotheism. This is because each of the three pillars represents one of Satan's attempts to prevent Abraham from sacrificing Ismail as proof of his faith in the only one true god. According to the legend the devout trio countered the diabolic test by throwing pebbles. Ismael survived, as is well known, his father sacrificed a ram in his place and the sacrificing of animals replaced the human sacrifice.

Abraham's preparedness to kill is still remembered today as the most important day in the Islamic world. It coincides with the Hajj and is celebrated right after the stoning of the devil near the Jamarat Bridge. However, where once the ritual of slaughtering of a sheep marked the climax of the day, today outsourcing with a required fee is more the order of the day, one *has* the sheep slaughtered if at all. The first Jamarat Bridge was a life-threatening place where the sacrifice of animals as in the story of Abraham was voluntarily substituted with the human sacrifice.

Admittedly the Hajj has always fundamentally been an undertaking involving the preparedness to die. Ali Schariati describes this especially vividly: "Before the pilgrimage settle debts, cleanse the mind of discord, subdue anger, bring daily life and finances in order and then pronounce your death as if never to return from the journey you are about to start."[121] He continues: "Practise dying, die before you die, choose now death symbolically! Resolve to die, take leave of this world! Set off on the pilgrimage!"[122]

Since the 9th century Islamic legal practitioners have divided the world in two, namely into the 'House of Islam' (*Dar al-Islam*) and the 'House of War' (*Dar al-Harb*). A state of war will reign between these two houses until the 'House of War' no longer exists and Islam has won the day.[123] This war, as is well-known, is called the Jihad and Mecca can be considered to be its stern Muslim home front. Ever since the time of Mohammed non-believers are not allowed to enter Mecca, Mina and the surrounding area. A longer border stretches round this sacred territory. Although only a few control posts safeguard the Islamic purity of the city, e.g. on the motorway from Jeddah to Mecca, non-Muslims are strongly advised to use an alternative route called the 'Christian bypass' [Fig. 22].

Deep in the heart of the 'House of Islam' the pillars of the devil at the Jamarat Bridge form, like a matryoshkan doll, a symbolic 'House of War', and it is here that the Jihad is rehearsed in a ritualised form. "On ... the day of sacrifice the battle begins."[124] Then: "Each soldier in Abraham's camp must shoot 70 bullets at the enemy in Mina. He must aim at the enemy's head,

---

[121] Ali Schariati: *Hadsch*, Bonn: Botschaft der Islamischen Republik Iran, 1983, p. 16.
[122] Ibid.
[123] Quran: Sure 8, 39 und 9, 41.
[124] Schariati, *Hadsch*, p. 69.

Fig. 22: Sacred territory: Motorway sign near Mecca.

chest or heart."[125] Those who are not such good shots should collect enough pebbles to compensate for his shortcomings in this field, and the ammunition must not run out on any account: "There is no peace at the front in Mina."[126]

A new Jamarat Bridge costing US$ 1.1 billion has been under construction since 2006 [Fig. 23]. According to the plans of the offices of Al-Handasah Shair & Partners in Cairo an enormous five-storey building allowing the flow of 100,000 people per hour per storey will be the result. In comparison the Wembley Stadium holds 90,000 people. Each storey will have a length of 600 metres and a width of nearly 100 metres. On completion in the year 2009 three million pilgrims will be able to perform the ritual of stoning every day from sunrise to sunset. As if that was not enough, as of 2009 it is planned to increase the bridge's capacity by adding a further five storeys. By the year 2015 six

---

[125] Ibid., p 70.
[126] Ibid.

Fig. 23: 100,000 people per hour per storey: The new Jamarat Bridge, under construction since 2006.

million pilgrims are expected to be able to cross the bridge every day; this approximates the total population of Israel.

One can undoubtedly assume that the new Jamarat Bridge will be as safe as 'Abraham's bosom'. It will be the paradigm of exit-architecture, an anti-panic construction wherever one looks. The place where human sacrifice turned to animal sacrifice and back again will no longer claim any more lives.

Niklas Luhmann was completely convinced that evolutionary theory is not able to provide the basis for prognosis. It does not allow the interpretation of the future but merely explains structural alterations.[127] But the more we learn about cultural evolution through transmission theory the clearer it becomes that where stress vanishes enculturation vanishes too. With the building of the new Jamarat Bridge the preparedness to die will vanish and the Hajj will become nothing more than a metaphysical wellness holiday. Thus the new Jamarat Bridge could turn out to be a secularisation machine – an epoch-making masterpiece of unconscious *Intelligent Design*.

4. 5 Codes: Space of Conflict (The Temple of Janus Revisited, Washington D.C., 2009)

With the pervasiveness of war two basic binarities of thought have gone missing: that of interior and exterior as well as that of war and peace. These have been superseded by 'military confrontation', 'transgressive use of violence' and 'operations'; and, above all: *conflict*. There is no form of peace which can viably stand in opposition to war. "Such conceptual quakings not only herald a seismographic epoch-making shift but also changes in the self-description which creates epochs."[128] In his *Leviathan* Thomas Hobbes once described: "A time where no war is being waged is called peace." Also Carl von Clausewitz wrote with a good conscience in his work that, the purpose of war is peace and as soon as this had been achieved then 'the business of war'

---

[127] Cf. Niklas Luhmann: *Die Gesellschaft der Gesellschaft*, Frankfurt am Main: Suhrkamp, 1997, p. 429.

[128] Niels Werber: "Krieg und Frieden: Ein Beben der Begriffe", in: *Frankfurter Rundschau*, 2 February 2007.

ceases. However, the numerous non-wars of the present put an end to those times where everything was so clearly definable.

Since its birth, military theory has warned us of the cities. Wars in urban areas should be avoided under any circumstances. However, with the paradigm of pervasiveness bellicose conflicts have for the most part been relocated into the cities. Architects find themselves and their work increasingly at the centre of existential conflicts. Thus for example architects working under the auspices of Israel's resettlement policies in West Jordan have to put up with being accused of being 'war criminals'.[129] Apparently it is no longer possible to dichotomise architecture into *architectura militaris* (engineering) and *architectura civilis* (architecture).

A siege was still warfare on the city's *perimeter*, urban warfare on the other hand is war *inside* the cities. For the latter no clearer difference can be hoped for between internal and external. The roots of urban warfare can be found in the 19th century in diffuse regions bordering on expanding colonial empires. There, in the fights of colonial armies with telluric partisans,[130] the city became for the first time the scene of warfare.[131] For example in Algiers in 1840, French troops under Marshall Burgeaud saw themselves faced with 'inner enemies' which could no longer be fought using traditional methods thereby creating a principle for town planning that was soon to make great strides: the selective destruction of whole quarters. The most famous recipi-

---

[129] Cf. Eyal Weizman: "The Evil Architects Do", in: Rem Koolhaas (ed.): *Content*, Cologne: Taschen, 2004, pp. 60-63.

[130] On the "telluric character" of the partisan see Carl Schmitt (1963): *Theorie des Partisanen. Zwischenbemerkung zum Begriff des Politischen*, Berlin: Dunker & Humblot, 2002, and Herfried Münkler: *Der Partisan. Theorie, Strategie, Gestalt*, Wiesbaden: VS Verlag für Sozialwissenschaften, 1990.

[131] Cf. "Krieg der Städte – Eyal Weizman im Gespräch mit Philipp Misselwitz", in: *ARCH+*, No. 164/165, April 2003, p. 64.

ent of Burgeaud's approach was Georges-Eugène Haussmann, who in 1853 was appointed as Prefect of the Département de la Seine by Napoleon III and redesigned the face of Paris so that government troops could, at any time, convert the magnificent boulevards into a battleground where they would have a clear field of fire. "The French army's antiurban experiments coincide with the beginnings of modern town planning."[132]

The French colonial army found itself exposed to tactics which anticipated the asymmetric warfare of the 21st century.[133] Urban regions play a key role in conflicts which have been prevalent since the end of the Cold War. Today's fighting in the streets differs from traditional warfare on the battlefield above all by the addition of the third dimension. The old battlefields were easy to supervise whereas, in an Arabian Medina, not only is it impossible to keep track of what is going on but any technological superiority is lost.[134] In order to fight against an American military hegemony its enemies have withdrawn into the complex, multi-storey, vertical terrain of the city and its surroundings.[135] Tariq Azis, Iraq's former Foreign Minister said in 2002: "Some people say to me the Iraqis are not the Vietnamese! They have no jungles or swamps to hide in. I reply, 'Let our cities be our swamps and our building our jungles.'"[136] As a reaction to these developments a military strategic city exploration occurred which remained unobserved for a long time.[137]

---

[132] Ibid.

[133] Ibid., p. 65.

[134] Stephen Graham: "Introduction: Cities, Warfare and State of Emergency", in: Stephen Graham (ed.): *Cities, War, and Terrorism*, Malden/Oxford/Victoria: Blackwell 2004, p. 19.

[135] Graham, "Introduction: Cities, Warfare and State of Emergency", p. 20.

[136] Quoted after Graham, "Introduction: Cities, Warfare and State of Emergency", p. 18.

[137] Cf. ibid.

This is the setting for a project, that is to be implemented in Washington D.C. in January 2009, that is to say during the first 100 days of the new US presidency: the *5 Codes: Space of Conflict*. This space takes the form of a reincarnation of the Roman Temple of Janus. In contrast to its model of old however, *5 Codes: Space of Conflict* abstains from distinguishing between open and closed i.e. war and peace. Committed to all other intermediate levels beyond these two extremes the *5 Codes: Space of Conflict* is above all a temporary architecture between a department store and a political forum.

With the advent of the new wars 'things' have moved into our field of awareness more than ever before. An array of low-tech products such rucksacks, carpet knives, soles of shoes, containers for liquids and so on have for some time now posed a considerable threat. Also high-tech products like iPods and other gadgets are inconceivable without the power of innovation which is to improve a MOUT agent's or IDF soldier's chances of survival.

Bruno Latour is right when he points out that it is always political science oddly enough that falls silent as soon as objects turn up.[138] It is here that etymology sheds some light on the roots of things in political matters as the word 'thing' or in German 'Ding' originally meant an archaic assembly. Even today this can be found in the names of Nordic parliaments: In Norway members of congress meet in the Storting and Icelandic delegates, the equivalent of 'thinghumans', assemble in the Althing. Many other examples can be found. "Long before it referred to an object thrown out of the political sphere which was outside objective and independent, the word 'thing' or 'Ding' referred to something which brought people together because it divided them."[139]

---

[138] Bruno Latour: *Von der Realpolitik zur Dingpolitik*, Berlin: Merve, 2005, p. 13.
[139] Latour, *Von der Realpolitik zur Dingpolitik*, pp. 29-30.

Many things put to use in the new wars are held together by the electromagnetic spectrum, and it must have been some special kind of intuition which led to the Bush administration choosing of all things a terrorist warning system based on the colours of the visible part of this spectrum. The Homeland Security Advisory System, presented in March 2002 by Tom Ridge, the Homeland Security Advisor at that time, defines five levels of danger: Code Green, Code Blue, Code Yellow, Code Orange and Code Red – known as the *5 Codes*.[140] Between war (Code Red) and peace (Code Green) lies a colourful spectrum of fear. Thus five colours stand for all possible graduations between war and peace. The image represents a suggestive icon of the state of emergency. Even though the sequence of colours does not correspond to the increasing wave lengths of the colours of the spectrum (blue comes 'before' green) the motif of the rainbow is all the same a wise choice by the US government as it was the "Rainbow Warrior" Isaac Newton who with his prismatic analysis of "white divine light" made a major contribution to the dawn of the age of risk. As in the case of visible light which is only tiny sector of the much larger invisible electromagnetic spectrum, the *5 Codes* too, represent the invisible risks associated with US-American orientations.

In the form of public debates and product shows the *5 Codes: Space of Conflict* enquires about the *decorum* of the present. This is to be found, or that is the way it is presented, in the sum of all preference traits of commodity artefacts. If successful, i.e. if memoactive design is identical, for the main part, with the amnesis of success in war and military technology then is it possible to have Code-Yellow preferences and Code-Yellow artefacts? Might there be Code-Blue, Code-Orange and Code-

---

[140] Cf. Igmade (eds.), *5 Codes: Architecture, Paranoia and Risk in Times of Terror*.

Green products?[141] Are only indicator traits to be found in the sector 'Code Red' or are there also preference traits there, too?

The prototype of all parliaments – the Palace of Westminster – is not airy, light-suffused, grove with Greek columns, but a cramped, dark and uncomfortable pit lined with benches which regularly puts parliamentarians under stress. "Are not all parliaments not only by the nature of the thing itself but also by the roar of the overcrowded thing, divided?"[142] It is this overcrowded thing called the 'House of Commons Chamber' which brought us to the realization that the things we shape, shape us, too. It is only when the things do not suit us that we become aware of them. Only then can a thing's proximity to war or peace, architecture or the design of a product be located in a spectrum which also includes the visible light of the *5 Codes*.

---

[141] Cf. Mühlmann, "The Economics Machine", p. 237.
[142] Latour, *Von der Realpolitik zur Dingpolitik*, p. 30.

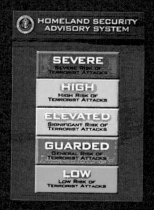

5 Codes: Space of Conflict (Tempel of Janus Revisited)

Project, Washington D.C., 2009

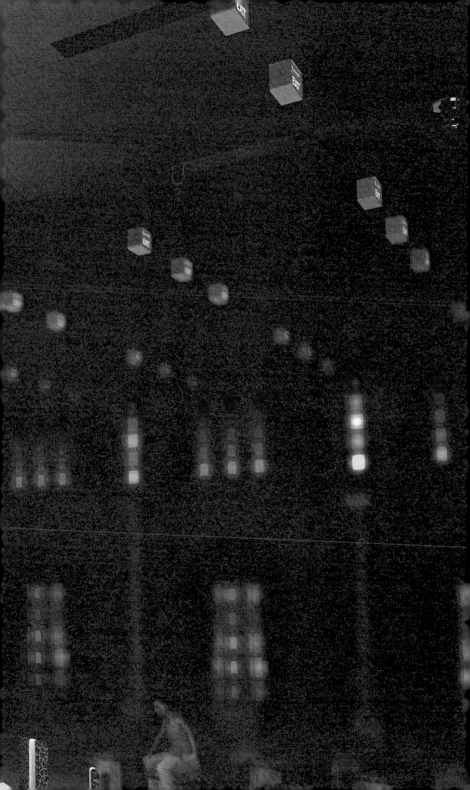

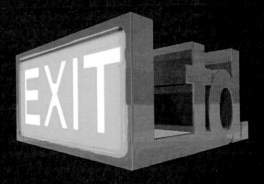

Architecture:
Exit Ltd.: Stephan Trüby, Julian Friedauer,
Stephan Henrich, Iassen Markov

Bibliography

Agamben, Giorgio (2002): *Homo sacer. Die souveräne Macht und das nackte Leben*, Frankfurt am Main: Suhrkamp.

Aicher, Otl, Jürgen Becker and Wolfgang Pehnt (1990): *Zugänge – Ausgänge*, photos by Timm Rautert, Cologne: Verlag der Buchhandlung Walther König.

Arkoun, Mohamed (1978): "Der Haddsch im islamischen Denken", in: Mohamed Ben Smail (ed.): *Pilgerfahrt nach Mekka*, Zurich/Freiburg im Breisgau: Atlantis.

Asendorf, Christoph (1989): *Ströme und Strahlen. Das langsame Verschwinden der Materie um 1900*, Gießen: Anabas.

Aunger, Robert (ed.; 2001): *Darwinizing Culture: The Status of Memetics As a Science*, Oxford/New York: Oxford University Press.

Banham, Reyner (1960): *Theory and Design in the First Machine Age*, London: The Architectural Press.

Bevan, Robert (2006): *The Destruction of Memory: Architecture at War*, London: Reaktion Books.

Böhme, Hartmut (2006): *Fetischismus und Kultur. Eine andere Theorie der Moderne*, Reinbek bei Hamburg: Rowohlt.

Bolz, Norbert (2006): *Bang-Design. Design-Manifest des 21. Jahrhunderts*, Hamburg: Trendbüro.

Bonß, Wolfgang (1995): *Vom Risiko: Unsicherheit und Ungewißheit in der Moderne*, Hamburg: Hamburger Edition.

Bourdieu, Pierre (1998): "Kode und Kodifizierung", in: Johanna Hofbauer, Gerald Prabitz and Josef Wallmannsberger (eds.): *Bilder, Symbole, Metaphern. Visualisierung und Informierung in der Moderne*, Vienna: Passagen.

Boyd, Robert and Peter J. Richerson (1985): *Culture and the Evolutionary Process*, University of Chicago Press, Chicago.

Boyd, Robert and Peter J. Richerson (2005): *The Origin and Evolution of Cultures*, Oxford/New York: Oxford University Press.

Butler, Samuel (1877): *Life and Habit*.

Brock, Bazon and Gerlinde Koschik (eds.; 2002): *Krieg + Kunst*, Munich: Wilhelm Fink.

Brock, Bazon (2002): "Säkularisierung der Kulturen", in: Bazon Brock and Gerlinde Koschik (eds.): *Krieg + Kunst*, Munich: Wilhelm Fink.

Burchett, Bessie Rebecca (1918): *Janus in Roman Life and Cult. Studies in Roman Religion*, Menasha, Wisconsin: George Banta.

Cicero (55 BC): *De oratore, II*.

Deleuze, Gilles and Félix Guattari (1980): *A Thousand Plateaus*, Minneapolis: University of Minnesota Press, 1987.

Deleuze, Gilles (1990): "Postskriptum über die Kontrollgesellschaften", in: Gilles
    Deleuze: *Unterhandlungen 1972-1990*, Frankfurt am Main: Suhrkamp.
Dennett, Daniel (1995): *Darwin's Dangerous Idea*, London: Penguin.
Duffy, Christopher (1979): *Siege Warfare: The Fortress in the Early Modern World
    1494-1660*, London/New York: Routledge.
Dunne, Anthony (2005): *Hertzian Tales: Electronic Products, Aesthetic Experience, and
    Critical Design*, Cambridge, Mass./London: The MIT Press.
Dünne, Jörg and Stephan Günzel (eds.; 2006): *Raumtheorie: Grundlagentexte aus
    Philosophie und Kulturwissenschaften*, Frankfurt am Main: Suhrkamp.

Elias, Norbert (1939): *Über den Prozeß der Zivilisation. Soziogenetische und psycho-
    genetische Untersuchungen*, Vol. 1, Frankfurt am Main: Suhrkamp, [18]1993.
Erdheim, Mario (1997): "Einleitung: Freuds Erkundungen an den Grenzen zwischen
    Theorie und Wahn", in: Sigmund Freud: *Zwei Fallberichte*, Frankfurt am
    Main: Fischer, 1997.
Evans, Robin (1978): "Figures, Doors, Passages", in: *Translations from Drawing to
    Building and Other Essays*, London: AA Publications, 1996.

Flusser, Vilém: "Vom Vater aller Dinge" (http://www.khm.de/flusser/material.html).
Forty, Adrian (1986): *Objects of Desire: Design and Society since 1750*, London:
    Thames & Hudson.
Forty, Adrian (2000): *Words and Buildings. A Vocabulary of Modern Architecture*, New
    York: Thames & Hudson.
Foucault, Michel (1975): *Discipline and Punish: The Birth of the Prison*, London:
    Penguin, 1977.
Freud, Sigmund (1911, 1923): *Zwei Fallberichte*, Frankfurt am Main: Fischer, 1997.

Ganschow, Thomas (2007): *Krieg in der Antike*, Darmstadt: Primus.
Goffman, Erving (1961): *Asylums. Essays on the Social Situation of Mental Patients
    and Other Inmates*, New York: Doubleday Anchor.
Graham, Stephen (2004): "Introduction: Cities, Warfare and State of Emergency", in:
    Stephen Graham (ed.): *Cities, War, and Terrorism*, Malden/Oxford/Victoria:
    Blackwell. ·
Grunwald, Thomas (2006): "Kognitive Module und modulare Prozesse. Ein Vorwort",
    in: Heiner Mühlmann: *Jesus überlistet Darwin*, Vienna/New York: Springer.
Günther, Hubertus (1988): "Die Kriegskunst in der Renaissance", in: Hubertus
    Günther (ed.): *Deutsche Architekturtheorie zwischen Gotik und Renaissance*,
    Darmstadt: Wissenschaftliche Buchgesellschaft.

Hammoudi, Abdellah (2005): *A Season In Mecca: Narrative Of A Pilgrimage*,
    Cambridge: Polity Press, 2006.
Hays, K. Michael (1998): *Architecture Theory since 1968*, Cambridge, Mass./London:
    The MIT Press.

Heinen, Ulrich (2002): "Friedenssehnsucht als Antrieb der europäischen Weltfriedenskupltur: Vergils Aeneis und Europa", in: Brock, Bazon and Gerlinde Koschik (eds.): *Krieg + Kunst*, Munich: Wilhelm Fink.

Helbing, Dirk, Ilés Farkas and Tamás Vicsek: "Simulating dynamical features of escape panic", in: *Nature*, Vol. 407, 28 September 2000.

Helbing, Dirk, Anders Johansson and Habib Zein Al-Abideen (2007): "The Dynamics of Crowd Disasters: An Empirical Study", in: *Physical Review* E 75, 046109 (arxiv.org/pdf/physics/0701203).

Hofbauer, Johanna, Gerald Prabitz and Josef Wallmannsberger (eds.; 1998): *Bilder, Symbole, Metaphern. Visualisierung und Informierung in der Moderne*, Vienna: Passagen.

Hoyer, Johann Gottfried von (1817-18): *Allgemeines Wörterbuch der Kriegsbaukunst*, 3 Vol., Berlin.

Igmade (eds.; 2006): *5 Codes: Architecture, Paranoia and Risk in Times of Terror*, Basel/Boston/Berlin: Birkhäuser.

Kaulbach, Hans-Martin (1998): "Peter Paul Rubens: Diplomat und Maler des Friedens", in: *1648: Krieg und Frieden in Europa*, Vol. II: Kunst und Kultur, exhibition catalogue, Münster.

"Friedrich Kittler und Alexander Kluge im Gespräch mit der ARCH+: Das Arsenal der Architektur" (2003), in: *ARCH+* No. 164/165: "Das Arsenal der Architektur", April 2003.

Kittler, Friedrich (2002): "Von Städtern und Nomaden", in: Bazon Brock and Gerlinde Koschik (eds.): *Krieg + Kunst*, Munich: Wilhelm Fink.

Kohl, Karl-Heinz (2003): *Die Macht der Dinge: Geschichte und Theorie sakraler Objekte*, Munich: C. H. Beck.

Krause, Detlef ([3]2001): *Luhmann-Lexikon*, Stuttgart: Lucius & Lucius.

Laplanche, Jean and Jean-Bertrand Pontalis (1972): *Das Vokabular der Psychoanalyse*, Frankfurt am Main: Suhrkamp.

Latour, Bruno (2005): *Von der Realpolitik zur Dingpolitik*, Berlin: Merve.

Le Corbusier (1929): *1929 – Feststellungen zu Architektur und Städtebau*, Bauwelt Fundamente 12, Braunschweig/Wiesbaden: Vieweg, 1987.

Lewin, Kurt (1917): "Kriegslandschaft" in: Jörg Dünne and Stephan Günzel (eds.): *Raumtheorie: Grundlagentexte aus Philosophie und Kulturwissenschaften*, Frankfurt am Main: Suhrkamp, 2006.

Luhmann, Niklas (1997): *Die Gesellschaft der Gesellschaft*, Frankfurt am Main: Suhrkamp.

Luhmann, Niklas (2003): *Soziologie des Risikos*, Berlin/New York: de Gruyter.

Marx, Karl (1867): *Das Kapital*, Erster Band, Marx-Engels-Werke No. 23, Berlin/DDR: Dietz, 1956.

Miessgang, Thomas (2003): "Pixelparade in der Feuerwüste", in: *Attack! Kunst und Krieg in den Zeiten der Medien*, exhibition catalogue, ed. by Kunsthalle Wien, Göttingen: Steidl.

Mitchell, Edward (2004): "Fear Factors", in: *Perspecta 35: Building Codes*, Cambridge, Mass.: The MIT Press.

Mühlmann, Heiner (1996): *The Nature of Cultures. A Blueprint for a Theory of Culture Genetics*, Vienna/New York: Springer.

Mühlmann, Heiner (1998): *Kunst und Krieg – Das säuische Behagen in der Kultur (Heiner Mühlmann über Bazon Brock)*, Cologne: Salon Verlag.

Mühlmann, Heiner (2005): *MSC. Maximal Stress Cooperation: The Driving Force of Cultures*, Vienna/New York: Springer.

Mühlmann, Heiner (^{2}2005): *Ästhetische Theorie der Renaissance. Leon Battista Alberti*, Bochum: Marcel Dolega.

Mühlmann, Heiner (2006): "The Economics Machine", in: Igmade (eds.): *5 Codes: Architecture, Paranoia and Risk in Times of Terror*, Basel/Boston/Berlin: Birkhäuser.

Mühlmann, Heiner (2007): *Jesus überlistet Darwin*, Vienna/New York: Springer.

Münkler, Herfried (1990): *Der Partisan. Theorie, Strategie, Gestalt*, Wiesbaden: VS Verlag für Sozialwissenschaften.

Münkler, Herfried (2003): "Die Neuen Kriege", in: *ARCH+*, No. 164/165, April 2003.

Münkler, Herfried (2005): *Über den Krieg: Stationen der Kriegsgeschichte im Spiegel ihrer theoretischen Reflexion*, Weilerswist: Velbrück.

Neumann, Hartwig (1988): *Festungsbaukunst und Festungsbautechnik. Deutsche Wehrbauarchitektur vom XV. bis XX. Jahrhundert*, Koblenz: Bernard & Graefe.

Nietzsche, Friedrich (1882): *The Gay Science.*

Pawley, Martin (1990): *Theory and Design in the Second Machine Age*, Oxford/Cambridge, Mass.: Blackwell.

Pehnt, Wolfgang (1990): "Drinnen und draußen: Splitter und Späne zur Geschichte der Tür", in: Otl Aicher, Jürgen Becker and Wolfgang Pehnt: *Zugänge – Ausgänge*, photos by Timm Rautert, Cologne: Verlag der Buchhandlung Walther König.

Philipp, Klaus Jan (1999): "Normierung 'avant la lettre'. Eine Blütenlese", in: Walter Prigge (eds.): *Ernst Neufert – Normierte Baukultur*, Frankfurt am Main: Campus.

Prigge, Walter (ed.; 1999): *Ernst Neufert – Normierte Baukultur*, Frankfurt am Main: Campus.

Rasch, Bodo (1980): *Zeltstädte*, IL 29, Stuttgart: Karl Krämer.

Rapaille, Clotaire (2006) *The Culture Code: An Ingenious Way to Understand Why People Around the World Live and Buy as They Do*, New York: Broadway.

Raulet, Gérard (2003): "Ornament", in: *Historisches Wörterbuch der Rhetorik*, ed. by Gert Ueding, Tübingen: Max Niemeyer.

Robnik, Drehli and Siegfried Mattl (2003): "'No one else is gonna die!' Urban warriors und andere Ausnahmefälle in neuen Kriegen und Blockbustern", in: *Attack! Kunst und Krieg in den Zeiten der Medien*, exhibition catalogue, ed. by Kunsthalle Wien, Göttingen: Steidl.

Schariati, Ali (1983): *Hadsch*, Bonn: Botschaft der Islamischen Republik Iran.

Schmitt, Carl (1922): *Politische Theologie*.

Schmitt, Carl (1963): *Theorie des Partisanen. Zwischenbemerkung zum Begriff des Politischen*, Berlin, 2002.

Schröder, Dorothea (1998): *Zeitgeschichte auf der Opernbühne. Barockes Musiktheater in Hamburg im Dienst von Politik und Diplomatie (1690-1745)*, Göttingen: Vandenhoeck & Ruprecht.

Seeßlen, Georg (1994): "War Rooms, Casinos & Gadgets: Die mythische Konstruktion der Bauten von Ken Adam", in: Jürgen Berger (ed.): *Ken Adam. Production Design, Meisterwerke der Filmarchitektur*, Munich/Mannheim: SFK-Verband and Landesmuseum für Technik und Arbeit.

Smail, Mohamed Ben (ed.; 1978): *Pilgerfahrt nach Mekka*, Zurich/Freiburg im Breisgau: Atlantis.

Störig, Hans Joachim (1992): *Kleine Weltgeschichte der Philosophie*, Frankfurt am Main: Fischer.

Trüby, Stephan (2005): "FAQ IGMADE. *Antworten auf Fragen zur igmade archplus 171 und zum Label igmade*", in: *ARCH+* No. 12/2005.

Trüby, Stephan (2006): "5 Codes: Architecture, Paranoia and Risk", in: Igmade (eds.): *5 Codes: Architecture, Paranoia and Risk in Times of Terror*, Basel/Boston/Berlin: Birkhäuser.

Trüby, Stephan (2007): "ESWTNJB - Notes for a Conspiracy-theoretical Architecture Novel", in: *Die Planung/A Terv*, Budapest/Berlin.

Tzonis, Alexander and Liane Lefaivre (1987): *Das Klassische in der Architektur. Die Poetik der Ordnung*, Bauwelt Fundamente 72, Braunschweig: Vieweg.

Viel, Hans-Dieter (2002): *Der Codex Hammurapi*, Göttingen: Duehrkohp + Radicke.

Vidler, Anthony (1977): "The Third Typology", in: K. Michael Hays: *Architecture Theory since 1968*, Cambridge, Mass./London: The MIT Press, 1998.

Vogel, Steve (2007): *The Pentagon. A History*, New York: Random House.

Weber, Bruce H. and David J. Depew (eds.; 2003): *Evolution and Learning: The Baldwin Effect Reconsidered*, Cambridge, Mass.: The MIT Press.

Weiser, Mark: "The Computer for the 21st Century" (http://www.ubiq.com/hypertext/weiser/SciAmDraft3.html).

"Eyal Weizman im Gespräch mit Philipp Misselwitz: Krieg der Städte", in: *ARCH+* No. 164/165, April 2003.

111

Weizman, Eyal (2004): "The Evil Architects Do", in: Rem Koolhaas (ed.): *Content*, Cologne: Taschen.

Welsch, Wolfgang (1990): *Ästhetisches Denken*, Stuttgart: Reclam.

Welzer, Harald (2002): *Das kommunikative Gedächtnis. Eine Theorie der Erinnerung*, Munich: Beck.

Welzer, Harald and Hans J. Markowitsch (2006): "Reichweiten und Grenzen der interdisziplinären Gedächtnisforschung", in: Harald Welzer and Hans J. Markowitsch (eds.): *Warum Menschen sich erinnern können. Fortschritte der interdisziplinären Gedächtnisforschung*, Stuttgart: Klett-Cotta.

Werber, Niels (2007): "Krieg und Frieden: Ein Beben der Begriffe", in: *Frankfurter Rundschau*, 9 February 2007.

Picture Credits

Fig. 1: Archive Stephan Trüby.

Fig. 2: Archive Stephan Trüby.

Fig. 3: Hanno-Walter Kruft: *Geschichte der Architekturtheorie*.

Fig. 4: Archive Stephan Trüby.

Fig. 5: Archive Stephan Trüby.

Fig. 6: Archive Stephan Trüby.

Fig. 7: © Alena Meier.

Fig. 8: Archive Stephan Trüby.

Fig. 9: Archive Stephan Trüby.

Fig. 10: Archive Stephan Trüby.

Fig. 11: © Vincent Mazeau.

Fig. 12: Beatriz Colomina.

Fig. 13: Beatriz Colomina.

Fig. 14: Archive Stephan Trüby

Fig. 15: Ermitage, St. Petersburg.

Fig. 16: Archive Stephan Trüby

Fig. 17: Archive Stephan Trüby

Fig. 18: Archive Stephan Trüby

Fig. 19: Archive Stephan Trüby

Fig. 20: Archive Stephan Trüby

Fig. 21: Archive Stephan Trüby

Fig. 22: Archive Stephan Trüby

Fig. 23: Archive Stephan Trüby

About the Author

Stephan Trüby (b. 1970) is an architect, theoretician and curator who studied architecture at the AA School, London, where he also lectured. He is Professor of Architecture at the Karlsruhe University of Arts and Design (HfG). From 2001 to 2007 he was Assistant Professor for Architectural Theory and Design at Stuttgart University's IGMA, where he co-founded Igmade and directed its publications. He edited (with Gerd de Bruyn) *architektur_theorie.doc: Essays since 1960* (Birkhäuser, 2003) and *5 Codes: Architecture, Paranoia and Risk in Times of Terror* (Birkhäuser, 2006, ed. by Igmade). In 2008 Trüby edited *The World of Madelon Vriesendorp* (AA Publications, with Shumon Basar). He heads the architecture-, design- and consultancy firm Exit Ltd.